CBD $3.25   Sad

D0050988

The Return of a Mighty Church is inspirational, thought provoking and challenging. Jack Eggar has packed a lot into this little book. If your church has become unfocused, his practical step-by-step suggestions will help you to improve your church's vision.

Dr. John Ankerberg ✓
Host, *The John Ankerberg Show*
President, The Ankerberg Theological Research Institute

As I read Jack's book, *The Return of a Mighty Church*, I had a strange feeling of dejá vu. Seventeen years ago, I came to a church that had plateaued. I wish that I could have had this book as a tool. Both the story and the principles are wonderful resources for pastors trying to turn around or revive a church. I recommend it for pastors who have the courage to try.

John Bell
Senior Pastor, Grace Pointe Church
Naperville and Plainfield, Illinois

In *The Return of a Mighty Church,* Jack Eggar has struck a delightful balance of fun stories, practical principles and profound insights as he tells a story about the growth of a mighty church . . . A+, Jack!

Bobb Biehl
President, MasterplanningGroup.com

Jack Eggar absolutely nails one of the biggest challenges facing the Church today: In order to be effective, churches must find ways to focus on what is outside the church walls and impact their communities for Christ. Jack tells a fascinating and entertaining story that also packs a powerful message. This is a book that every pastor and church leader should read.

Reese Kauffman ✓
President, Child Evangelism Fellowship

If there ever was a day when we truly needed a *mighty church,* it is today. The church must take an honest look at the community surrounding it and become what God has purposed it to be.

Dave Meyers
Director of Development
New Tribes Mission Training Center

The Return of a Mighty Church

a modern fable

JACK EGGAR

Regal

From Gospel Light
Ventura, California, U.S.A.

PUBLISHED BY REGAL BOOKS
FROM GOSPEL LIGHT
VENTURA, CALIFORNIA, U.S.A.
PRINTED IN THE U.S.A.

Regal Books is a ministry of Gospel Light, a Christian publisher dedicated to serving the local church. We believe God's vision for Gospel Light is to provide church leaders with biblical, user-friendly materials that will help them evangelize, disciple and minister to children, youth and families.

It is our prayer that this Regal book will help you discover biblical truth for your own life and help you meet the needs of others. May God richly bless you.

For a free catalog of resources from Regal Books/Gospel Light, please call your Christian supplier or contact us at 1-800-4-GOSPEL *or* www.regalbooks.com.

Library of Congress Cataloging-in-Publication Data
Eggar, Jack.
   The return of a mighty church / Jack Eggar.
      p. cm.
   ISBN 0-8307-3895-9 (hard cover)
   1. Church renewal.   I. Title.
   BV600.3.E44 2005
   250—dc22   2005031256

1   2   3   4   5   6   7   8   9   /   10   09   08   07   06   05

Rights for publishing this book in other languages are contracted by Gospel Light Worldwide, the international nonprofit ministry of Gospel Light. Gospel Light Worldwide also provides publishing and technical assistance to international publishers dedicated to producing Sunday School and Vacation Bible School curricula and books in the languages of the world. For additional information, visit www.gospellightworldwide.org write to Gospel Light Worldwide, P.O. Box 3875, Ventura, CA 93006; or send an e-mail to info@gospellightworldwide.org.

To my beloved wife and ministry partner, Dona

Contents

Acknowledgments 9

Characters 10

Part One:
The Story of Midland Church

Chapter 1 12
A Comfortable Community

Chapter 2 22
A Personal Crisis

Chapter 3 32
The Visitor

Chapter 4 42
A Forgotten Document

Chapter 5 52
The Awakening

Chapter 6 67
The Original Vision

Chapter 7 77
The Five Rs

Chapter 8 99
Counting the Cost

Chapter 9 109
Outreach Tools

Chapter 10 121
Captain David

Chapter 11 135
Congregational Meeting

Chapter 12 147
Return to the Vision

Chapter 13 162
Community at Last

Part Two:
The Five Signposts at Work

Signpost 1 181

Rediscover Our Purpose

Signpost 2 184
Return to the Original Vision

Signpost 3 187
Rededicate the Church Family

Signpost 4 190
Reorganize Our Approach to the Community

Signpost 5 193
Remember

ACKNOWLEDGMENTS

My son-in-law Sam O'Neal played an integral role in
helping me bring to life the characters in this book.
He was given a tall order. An average church in
an average community struggling with the typical
problems every church faces was transformed into
a mighty church with true Kingdom vision and
passion. Sam is an assistant editor at *Christianity
Today* and his creativity enabled me to transfer
elements of a true story into the realm of what
possibly could happen in any church today.

Special thanks also to Awana communications
director Jim Jordan for his assistance in shaping the
antagonist. Every church has one! Steve Van Winkle,
a pastor in Montana in the midst of a big church
building project, and Dr. Greg Carlson, director
of the Rorheim Institute, helped me analyze the
manuscript from a biblical perspective. To this
team I give my heartfelt thanks.

CHARACTERS

Pastor David Newman:
New pastor of Midland Church

Catherine Newman:
Insightful wife of Pastor David

Ralph Nicholson:
Chairman of the elder board

Ken Siever:
Church consultant from Dallas, Texas

Terry Sullivan:
Church deacon

Sheryl Smith:
Outgoing Awana Commander

Dr. Daniel Newcomb:
Founding pastor of Midland Church

Mary Newcomb:
Hospitable wife of Dr. Newcomb

Fred Turner:
Church deacon and antagonist

PART ONE

The Story of Midland Church

CHAPTER 1

A Comfortable Community

Early morning rain fell softly on the blue Ford Taurus as David Newman guided it off the road and into the gravel parking lot. He made one exhausted loop around the property before stopping in front of a bent and rusted sign marked "Visitor." "Well, honey," he said, slipping the gearshift into park, "this is it—Midland Church."

By the look of its white wood siding, the small building they had traveled 2 days and almost 800 miles to find was fighting a losing battle against the forces of nature.

David stole a glance at his wife, who was using her sleeve to wipe condensation from the windshield.

"Catherine," he began hesitantly, "I know the building isn't much to look at. But it just needs a little bit of . . . personality . . . and . . . a lot of paint. Besides, you're going to absolutely love these people—" He would have stammered on if she hadn't quietly touched her finger to his lips.

"David," she said, smiling sweetly, "there's no need for a sales job. You're a godly man, and I trust your judgment." Her smile was contagious, and David found himself grinning from ear to ear as he reached under the seat for his umbrella.

"Well, then," he said, as he stepped out of the car and opened the umbrella, "let's take a look!"

Once inside the building, they were greeted by an average-sized man with an above-average-sized paunch, who identified himself as Fred Turner.

"It's very nice to finally meet you folks in person," Fred said. "Why don't you follow me, and we'll take a look around the place."

The inside of the church was surprisingly comfortable compared to the outside, and it didn't take David long to figure out that Fred had something to do with that. In fact, as David soon heard, Fred Turner was the Sunday School Superintendent, a deacon, a choir member, a teacher, the junior church director, and the general handyman around the property.

At the end of the tour, Fred led David and Catherine into a small cluster of rooms branching off from the entrance to the sanctuary.

"This here's the main office." Fred said. He gestured to a small, cramped room with a desk, two chairs and two large bookshelves. "And that there's the pastor's office. We figured you could prepare for the morning in there and see how you like it, since—" Fred broke off and rubbed the back of his neck, then continued, "since . . . you know . . . it'll be yours if everything goes okay."

"This will be great," David replied, giving his future colleague a hearty handshake. "By the way, Fred, were you a part of the pastoral search committee?"

Fred cocked his head a little to the left, as if considering the question from every angle before saying, "No sir, I did not have that pleasure. Actually, to be honest, I guess I thought we've been doing pretty well on our own." Fred turned on his heel and walked out of the office.

David and Catherine unconsciously joined hands in the center of the room.

"What do you suppose he meant by that?" David said.

Catherine shrugged, and then a smile spread across her face as she kissed him on the cheek.

"No time to worry about it now, *Pastor* David," she said. Her smile turned into a mischievous grin. "You've got a sermon to preach!"

Ralph Nicholson, board chairman for the Midland Church, loved church potluck dinners. He had organized a large number of them, including this one, and he looked around the room with a feeling of satisfaction. There was just something about the combination of food, friends and a lazy Sunday afternoon that always seemed to slow down the world just enough to bring out the best in people. Ralph stood up to address the congregation, still buzzing after David's sermon.

"Okay, ladies and gentlemen," he called to the crowd through an antique microphone, "we're about ready to start the meeting, so I recommend that y'all finish up with your meals." This comment started a small stampede in the direction of the dessert table.

"Before we get down to business," Ralph said, "I just want to say thank you to Reverend Newman for that wonderful sermon." He caught David's eye and winked. "I felt blessed by it, brother David, and I'm sure everyone here feels the same." There was a burst of applause and a few whistles from the back of the fellowship hall.

David, who was sitting at the head table with Catherine, stood up and made a clumsy half-bow that produced more than a few cheerful chuckles. As he sat back down, Catherine noticed once again the joyous smile that had been stamped across his face ever since he had preached that morning.

This is where God wants us, she said to herself and gave her husband's arm an encouraging squeeze. *This is where we belong.* The thought filled her with a peculiar excitement, and it wasn't long before she felt a similar smile start to light up her own face.

After a few minutes had passed (and the dessert table had been ransacked), Ralph picked up the old microphone and said, "All right, folks, let's go ahead and mosey back to the sanctuary. We've still got a lot of work to do today."

This announcement was followed by screeching chairs and clanging dishes as the entire congregation filed its way back into the sanctuary.

"Isn't this great?" David whispered to Catherine. "It felt so good to preach this morning! The Lord just seemed to confirm His approval while I preached. How do you feel?"

Catherine squeezed his hand, basking in his excitement.

When they had almost reached the sanctuary, David stopped and pulled Catherine close. He looked into her eyes and brushed back a lock of her hair. "Whatever happens next, are you okay with this?"

"There's no need to worry, David," she replied. "This is where God wants us to be." With that, she gave him a quick kiss on the cheek and walked through the door. After a couple of deep breaths and a quick prayer, David followed.

The congregational meeting began exactly the way those kinds of meetings are supposed to begin. Ralph Nicholson reintroduced the Newman family and spoke about their experiences in ministry.

Then David and Catherine walked to the front of the sanctuary for a time of questions and answers. The congregation asked a variety of questions, ranging from the Newmans' favorite colors to their opinions on music styles. Other congregants sat silently and listened to the answers, simply content to have a pastor among them once again.

As the minutes turned into an hour and more, several of the elders attempted to steer the conversation toward weightier matters by asking David a number of theological questions. As Catherine listened to his answers, she couldn't help but be proud of the way each of his responses was rooted in biblical truth and commonsense.

"Lord, please help them all to see his godly spirit," she prayed under her breath, "and please show us Your will."

Ralph Nicholson, who was anxious for the church to officially approve David as their new pastor, started to stand up and announce that it was time to vote when a loud voice called out from the back of the sanctuary.

"I have a question for ya, Pastor," said the voice. It was Fred Turner. His tone had an edge to it that made everyone turn around and look at him.

Fred stood up, tugged at his belt buckle, and said, "What are your plans for our church, Pastor David?"

A wave of heads swiveled back to the front to focus on the pastor and await his answer.

"That's a great question, Fred," David said without hesitation. "Basically, the Bible is very clear about the shepherding role of a pastor—"

"With all due respect, Pastor Newman, that's not what I'm askin' ya." Fred's voice sounded even more flinty and cold. "What I want to know is where you plan on takin' this church if you were to become our pastor. You see, we've always had a certain way of doin' things around here, and I think we all need to know exactly where you intend to lead us." Fred slowly crossed his arms over his chest and sat down with a satisfied grunt.

David took a sip of water out of the plastic bottle on the podium and glanced at his wife. She gave him a secret thumbs-up sign.

Encouraged, David replied, "Well, Fred, at this point, I guess I don't plan on leading you anywhere!"

There were several gasps from the congregation, and Fred's jaw dropped like an unhinged garage door.

David took another long, deliberate sip from the water bottle and then said, "I can't be the one to determine where this church is supposed to go. Fred, if you're looking for a pastor who can use a lot of pretty words to tell you what he thinks a church is supposed do, I guarantee you won't have a hard time finding one. But I also guarantee that your church will end up useless."

Fred's jaw closed with an audible snap, and he didn't speak again.

"What I'm saying," David continued, "is that a pastoral candidate should not come into a church with his own plans and expectations alone. He must listen to the people and learn from them. I'm told that Midland Church is almost 40 years old. There must be a rich history here of God's mighty works and His people who have walked with Him."

David's voice softened, and he scanned the congregation. "As a church body, it's *your* responsibility to figure out where you want to go, and it's my responsibility to help you get there, using the principles in the Bible." David held up his copy of the Good Book for emphasis. "Midland Church can be a mighty fortress for Jesus Christ, but we will have to work together in order to get there."

He stepped back from the podium and waited, but there were no more comments or questions. A strange silence had filled the sanctuary, and the individual members of the crowd all seemed to be impressed with such wisdom and insight, as if to say "This fellow can see things deeply."

Finally, Ralph Nicholson cleared his throat and stood up. "Well, I think that's enough excitement for one night," he said, still somewhat dazed himself. "I call for a motion from the floor to vote on extending a call to Rev. David Newman." The motion was called and seconded, and David and Catherine were asked to leave the sanctuary for the official vote. Once outside, Catherine jumped into her husband's arms and hugged him fiercely.

"I'm so proud of you, honey!" she exclaimed. "You were wonderful!"

"I don't know what came over me," David replied. "I just know I was telling the truth."

After about an hour had passed, Ralph Nicholson opened the door and stepped out into the hall.

"Well," he said, an enormous grin on his face, "congratulations, Pastor David Newman!" He slapped David on the back hard enough to make him stumble, and then caught him in a bear hug. "The vote was 65 in favor, and only 4 opposed! Let's go back in and greet your new congregation!"

David and Catherine joined hands and stepped back inside the door of the sanctuary to a round of wild applause. The Newmans returned to the podium and gracefully thanked the people for their kindness and then went to stand by the door to greet each member of the church individually. Fred Turner was nowhere to be seen.

Finally, excited and exhausted, nervous and happy, the couple drove back to their hotel and collapsed into bed.

That night, while David dreamed about his new church and about all of the ways he wanted to make a difference for the kingdom of God, his wife lay awake. She thought of the four votes against their call and wondered what that would mean in the weeks and months ahead. Surely Fred Turner had been one of those voters, and apparently three others felt the same way.

She reminded herself that good pastors seldom had everyone on their side. Why, men of action caused friction! Sixty-one out of 65 votes was entirely acceptable, she reasoned. But still she tossed and turned for several hours before finally praying herself to sleep.

CHAPTER 2

A Personal Crisis

David accepted his call to become pastor of the Midland Church at the beginning of January. By the middle of March, he was fully immersed in the community and culture of the church.

He enjoyed every minute as a senior pastor and diligently prepared his sermons, always making sure that he preached only on the authority of the Word of God. From the start he had made himself known to the congregation through hospital visits, home visits, office visits and a variety of social activities that Catherine organized and hosted at their home. He even enjoyed the various board and committee meetings. David quickly won the respect and admiration of the leaders of the church.

But below the surface, he began to realize that something was wrong with Midland Church. The source of his unease wasn't something he could articulate or put his finger on, but it was there and it was real. It lurked beneath all of the activities of the church and clawed at the back of David's mind whenever he slowed down enough to think (and pray) about how things were really going.

"Something's missing," David said to his wife one cool Tuesday evening at the close of dinner. "I know something is missing, but I have no idea what it is."

"Well, where have you looked?" said Catherine. She gathered the dirty dishes and carried them over to the sink.

"What do you mean?" he asked, a slight scowl furrowing his brow.

"Well, if something's missing," Catherine replied, "don't you think you should go look for it?" She sloshed soapy water over a dish and scrubbed away at a particularly stubborn spot.

David opened his mouth in retort to what he had interpreted as flippancy, but then the truth of what she had said hit home and he gently bit his tongue.

"Do you think I should look around the church?" he asked as he walked over to the sink and began drying the dishes in the drainer.

"Why, don't ask me, suh," Catherine chirped in a Southern drawl, "ah'm just your lowly wife!"

"I'd rather treat you like a snotty-nosed kid!" he

exclaimed, dipping a freshly washed bowl back into the soapy water. "I think it's time for your bath!"

Catherine screeched with laughter as her husband chased her down the hall into the living room.

"Okay, okay, I give up!" she cried when David cornered her between the couch and the entertainment center. "I'll help you find whatever it is you're missing!"

Satisfied, David put the bowl down and took his wife in his arms. "I think the first thing we need to do is pray," he said.

From that evening on, David made a commitment to observe all the activities of the church—especially the ones he wasn't directly in charge of. He began this necessary but painfully monotonous process by paying a visit to each Sunday School class. He found nothing out of the ordinary: Kids came and left after going through the various planned activities; senior high students had their weekly Friday evening activity and Bible study; board and committee meetings were the same everywhere.

Catherine did a bit of sleuthing as well but came up with nothing strange or troublesome.

As in so many churches on a midweek night, there was an Awana program in session. Usually, a couple dozen kids and their leaders met each Wednesday evening for several hours in the church fellowship hall, which had been built to serve the larger attendance the church echoed from its past.

When David dropped in to observe, he was initially surprised to see a group of young boys running around a huge color-coded circle. Each of the boys had beanbags balanced precariously on their heads, which caused them to run with their backs as straight as arrows.

At one point, one of the beanbags slipped off of the boy who was carrying it, eliciting several groans from his teammates. However, when the boy picked it up and jogged back to them, they patted him on the back and yelled words of encouragement to him as he started over.

Within a few minutes, David was called away and did not return to complete his personal survey. His conclusion was that because the church did not meet midweek any longer, a kid's club where children came to play fun games was about as good as anything.

Throughout the rest of the week, David explored every nook and cranny of the church in an effort to solve the source of the feeling that oppressed his spirit. He sat in on choir practice and had a good time singing along, although he was certain that he would never be asked to fill a solo part in a church cantata. He ate dinner with the deacons on Thursday evening and joined a small-group session with the men's group. On Friday, he watched the softball team practice and then went bowling with the youth. He even joined the Saturday morning women's breakfast with Catherine. ("Just this once, ladies," he promised.)

When the week came to a close, David was forced to admit that he was no closer to solving the mystery than he had been on that Tuesday evening with his wife when he told her something was missing. To make matters worse, the sense of foreboding grew even stronger as the days passed. In fact, on the Saturday afternoon of that week of observation, he wasn't able to concentrate enough to finish preparing his sermon for the following morning.

That's the last straw! David said to himself, finally admitting that he needed help. He reached across the desk for his red stress-ball and began to squeeze. "Gonna pop you this time for sure," he said under his breath as he concentrated on squeezing the ball and then relaxing his grip.

Then something caught his attention on the corner of his desk—an advertisement in *Ministry Leadership* magazine. "Let us help!" it read. "We can take your church to the next level." David brushed several sheets of paper out of the way to read the rest of the ad and discovered that it was placed by a company located in

Dallas called Ministry Solutions. Intrigued, David picked up the phone and was about to dial the number when he heard a knock at his door.

"Hey there, Pastor David, you wanted to see me?" It was Ralph Nicholson.

"Hi, Ralph, come on in." Ralph opened the door and David gestured to the padded chair in front of his desk. "Have a seat."

As David watched the big man close the door and then move toward a chair, he was tempted to tell him everything. He wanted to talk about his strange feeling that something was wrong with the church, and about his unsuccessful attempts to find whatever was missing. But before he could speak, a small, quiet voice spoke up from the back of his mind. *Not now,* said the voice. *There will be another time.*

David had originally contacted Ralph concerning a separate issue that had been on his mind, so he decided to go ahead with what he had planned to say. Fortunately, this second issue was much more concrete and discernible than the first; but unfortunately, it involved Fred Turner.

"Ralph," David said, somewhat hesitantly, "I need to talk to you about Fred Turner." He paused to see if Ralph would voice any objections. When he did not, David continued, "I'm just a little concerned about how many ministries he's involved in."

Ralph raised his eyebrows in puzzlement, inviting David to elaborate.

"I'm just worried that he's spreading himself too thin," David said, letting out a long sigh. "I'm afraid that the quality of his ministries is suffering because he has so many of them. Do you understand what I'm saying?"

Ralph slowly nodded his head up and down. "You think ol' Fred's got his hand in too many pies, is that it?"

"Yes, that's exactly it!" David said, hoping that he had correctly understood the big man's vernacular.

"Just so you know, Pastor—" Ralph started, and then seemed hesitant to finish. "Well, it's just that Fred ain't the only person who comes to church any time the door is open. We got a lot of folks like that."

"Oh I agree," David said. "But Fred alone is in charge of most of the ministries he attends. I think that makes a big difference."

Ralph leaned back in his chair and laced his hands behind his head. He didn't speak for a moment, and David assumed that this was his thinking position. David was proud of the big man for thinking things through and not blindly accepting whatever David said.

After a minute or so, Ralph leaned forward and placed his chin on top of his fist. "Yeah, I guess I can see your point. He's responsible for a truckload of ministry. So, do you think I should ask Fred to step back a little bit?"

Once again, Ralph's hands swooped behind his head and he leaned back into his thinking position. After what seemed like a very long time to David, Ralph leaned forward again. But instead of speaking, he scooped up a pencil from David's desk and began to tap it against his cheek.

Smiling, David leaned back in his own chair and simply waited for his friend.

"I don't think you should ask him to do anything at the moment," Ralph finally said. Now it was David's turn to raise his eyebrows, and Ralph's turn to elaborate further.

"I'm not sure that you really understand Fred," Ralph said, looking directly into David's eyes. "He really is a good man who loves the Lord—"

"I know that!" David blurted. "I'm not saying that Fred isn't faithful or serious; I'm just saying—"

Ralph held up his hand and nodded his head slowly, showing that he understood.

"Let me finish," he said politely. "Fred loves the Lord, but he's also as stubborn as a one-eyed mule!" David wasn't sure why a one-eyed mule was any more stubborn than a two-eyed one, but he decided to let the big man speak without any further interruptions.

"If you're gonna convince Fred to lighten his load a little," Ralph said, "you're gonna have to take it slow." Suddenly his eyes popped wide open with inspiration. "It's like pushin' a tractor with a dead motor! If you try to do it by yourself right away, you won't go nowhere. You're gonna need a team of folks, and you're gonna have to rock it back and forth a few times before it'll start to budge." Satisfied, Ralph settled back into his thinking position and waited for David to respond.

"I guess you have a point," said David, although he didn't sound totally convinced.

"Trust me, Pastor. Fred does have too many ministries, but let's you and me work on a plan that will help both ol' Fred and the church." Ralph stood up and deposited David's pencil back into the cup on the desk. "I've known Fred a long time," he said. With no further conversation, he nodded good-bye and left David alone with his thoughts.

David's mind sifted through the conversation. His initial instinct was to ignore the board chairman's advice and call Fred right away to discuss his overloaded schedule. But in the end, David decided to trust Ralph's experience and familiarity with the man in question. Wisdom called for patience. David's greater priority was to serve and to earn the respect and love of the people before attempting to change them. *Good counsel, Ralph!* David thought to himself.

He wondered when that right moment would come—with the right people—to talk with Fred. He couldn't figure out what made a church turn over most ministries to one person. But then he reasoned that the majority of folks at Midland Church were only casually connected to the church. For the most part, few had any real responsibilities to speak of. Fred just happened to be the one willing to do it all.

"Can't push that tractor all by myself," David said under his breath as he began to tidy up his desk before leaving.

CHAPTER 3

The Visitor

On a nippy Friday evening toward the end of March, a lanky middle-aged man checked into the Midland Motel. He wore dusty jeans and a white cowboy hat that contrasted with his suntanned, weathered face. But the leather briefcase suggested more than a cowboy coming to town.

After a quick glance around his room to make sure everything was acceptable, the man walked down Main Street a few blocks to the Ponderosa Steak House. Before going inside, he stopped and turned his attention to a young man leaning against a nearby streetlight.

"Excuse me, could you tell me where Midland Church is?" he asked.

The young man straightened and took an unconscious step back. "No, I'm afraid I have no idea," he replied. He waited for the stranger to say more, but the man simply thanked him and entered the restaurant.

When the man had been seated at a small booth near the buffet, he told the waitress, "I'll start with a cup of coffee and a glass of water." She returned with the beverages, and he handed her the menu. But instead of ordering, he repeated his earlier question: "Would you mind telling me how to get to Midland Church?"

The waitress twirled a lock of hair around her finger as she thought for a moment but then shook her head.

"Nope, can't recall the church," she said.

"Well that's okay, Miss." He smiled at her as he said, "Does the buffet come with the prime rib?"

Throughout the course of his meal, the stranger found a way to speak with several of the diners—in the buffet line, while heading for the restroom—and at the end of each conversation he always asked the same question: "Can you tell me where I can find Midland Church?"

Each time he received the same kind of answer: "No, sir, never heard of it—sorry I can't help."

Disappointed and a little sad, the man finished his meal in silence, left a generous tip for the waitress and walked slowly back to the motel.

At exactly 11:00 A.M. the next morning, the tall man with the white cowboy hat and leather briefcase walked into Pastor David's office.

"Good morning, Pastor Newman," he said with a confident smile and offered his hand. "I'm Ken Siever from Ministry Solutions."

Excited, and just a bit nervous, David stood up and accepted the handshake, then gestured toward a chair. "Thank you so much for coming, Ken. Will you please have a seat?"

"Actually, I have something I want to show you," Ken replied. "Come with me." Without waiting for a response, he turned on his heel and left the office.

Amused and curious, David followed Ken through the church and outside across the gravel parking lot. When Ken finally stopped and turned to face David, they were standing on the corner of Kearney and 9th Avenue in the middle of the street.

"Your church spoke to me last night," Ken said with an air of solemnity. "Would you like to know what it said?"

"I sure would," David said, his interest piqued even more.

"Your church told me, 'I'm broken and I'm dying, so there's no need to come here.' "

David's amusement evaporated into confusion, and he almost lost his balance right there in the middle of the street.

"What do you mean? I don't think . . . I . . . you
. . ." David stammered as he tried to think of a
response. "Don't you think that's a little harsh?" he
finally said.

"Actually, no," replied Ken in a matter-of-fact
voice. "You asked me to come out here because you felt
that there was a problem with your church, and now
I'm simply confirming that you were correct."

"Yes, but—" David broke off speaking, still grap-
pling with this man's abruptness, then said, "But
Midland Church isn't dying. We do a lot of very good
things here!"

"I know," Ken replied. "You have Bible studies and
prayer meetings and youth groups and on and on—am
I right?"

David agreed, a wary look on his face.

"I had those in my church too," Ken said, "but
there was always something missing under the surface,
something that just didn't feel right. Sound familiar?"

David gulped. *How can this guy describe my pain and
confusion to a T, having just now arrived?* he thought.

"Can you tell me what it is?" David asked, speaking in little more than a whisper. "Can you tell me
what's missing?"

Ken smiled and put his hand on David's shoulder.

"I'll show you," he said, turning David back in the
direction of the church. "Can you please read the

church sign for me?" He pointed to the small painted board at the edge of the parking lot. David brought his hand to his forehead to shield his eyes from the sun's glare. After squinting hard he lowered his hand and shook his head no.

"It's too small," he said, "I can't read it."

"Exactly."

Feeling a little dizzy, David recommended they get out of the street before they were run over.

"Come this way," Ken said as he almost jogged toward another part of the church.

Once again, David reluctantly followed the stranger in the white cowboy hat. As they explored the grounds, Ken pointed out several unsightly blemishes and potentially dangerous situations. The paint on the building was peeling and chipped. A broken windowpane was covered with duct tape. The bushes along the front garden were untrimmed and had pieces of trash caught in the shrubs in several places. Even the railing alongside the front steps was wobbly and seemed as if it might splinter at any moment. The sidewalk was broken and raised in places and the parking lot was still gravel. How old was Midland Church?

Ken had a meticulous eye for detail. As he pointed out each flaw, David found himself growing more and more irritated. *What does this have to do with the people and ministry of Midland Church?* David asked himself.

"What do you think all of this says to the community around you?" Ken asked after they had finished their inspection.

"Slobs worship here?" David ventured.

Ken chuckled at David's choice of words, then his face sobered. "I'm afraid it's even more serious than that. Your building is telling this community, 'We don't really care what you think, because we don't really want you in here anyway.'"

"But that's not true!" David cried. "We want to bring in as many visitors as we can!"

"Do you? Let's sit down and talk about it."

As they walked back into David's office, Ken told him about his adventures at the Ponderosa the night before and the people he had met along the street, in the motel and at the gas station. Ken had actually canvassed the neighborhood for several hours before arriving at the church.

"Everyone with whom I came in contact had one thing in common. They had no idea this church even exists."

As soon as David heard those words, a wall crumbled in his mind and he made the connection that had avoided him for so long.

"Of course!" he cried, jumping up from his chair and pointing a finger toward the church sign outside. "That's the missing piece! These dear saints have become so inwardly focused that they've succeeded in almost disappearing from the community."

Ken watched David's epiphany with interest and pleasure, remaining silent.

"We have plenty of inside activities and plenty of inside ministry," David said, "but it's all for ourselves! We haven't been engaging the community at all!" David took a deep breath and braced himself against the wall of the office. "No wonder I felt so strongly that something was wrong—not only were we not pursuing the Great Commission, but this church chose to literally disconnect somewhere along the way."

David's words buzzed in mid-air like unseen hummingbirds for a moment and then slammed themselves back into his mind with enough force to knock the strength out of his knees and send him slumping back into his chair.

"We haven't obeyed the Great Commission," David said, this time in a horrified whisper. "I think we're dying. We just don't know it."

Ken reached out to give David a reassuring pat on the shoulder. "Don't worry, Pastor Newman," he said. "This church isn't dead yet. Besides, even if it were, that wouldn't stop Jesus, now, would it?" As he spoke, David could tell by the passion in the man's eyes that he really loved the Lord and wanted to serve Him. He could also tell that this strange visitor wanted the best for Midland Church.

"Well, then," David said, letting his pride slip to the floor like a discarded garment. "I'm ready to listen. How do we turn things around?"

"I'm afraid I'm fresh out of 'church in a can.' Would you like to try the microwave version instead?" Ken smiled gently and said more seriously, "I'm sorry. It's just that every church is a totally unique organism. If you're going to get things back on track, you're going to have to set up a plan specifically designed for your church alone."

David recognized the wisdom in this statement and leaned back in his chair to ponder its implications, then said, "How did you turn things around in your church?"

At first Ken didn't respond, but after a moment, the tall man sighed a slow, heavy release of emotion, and an expression that looked like a wince of pain shot across his features.

"We didn't turn things around," Ken said. "We died." As he spoke, his voice lost the solemn lightness that had so intrigued David at the beginning of their meeting. Now it sounded thick and almost choked. "I wandered around for a few years after we sold the building, kind of hopping from church to church, and I learned a few things. That's when I started Ministry Solutions. I wanted to help people avoid what I went through."

The two men sat in silence for a time—one wading through the pain of a failed past and the other sifting through the horrifying potential of a wasted future. Finally, Ken shook his head and pulled himself back into the present.

"Well, I've gotta run," he said, standing up quickly and collecting his briefcase.

"So soon?" David said. "I have so many things I want to ask you!"

"I have an appointment about 100 miles from here at four o'clock—but why don't you walk me to my car? I parked a few blocks away."

As they walked, the two men shared their experiences about the joys and frustrations of ministry. For David, it was exhilarating to encounter a man who understood the obstacles of ministry but seemed to be unfazed by them.

When Ken pointed out his rental car and fished the keys out of his pocket, a wave of oppression swept over David's heart. "I don't know what to do next!" he lamented aloud.

"Every church is started by someone with a vision for what might be," Ken said. "When that vision gets lost, the church begins to flatten and eventually dies. I'm afraid there's very little that Ministry Solutions can do for you at this stage. But don't give up! Let me suggest that you search for the reason your church was started. Then you can figure out how to raise the church out of this place of perpetual mediocrity and isolation from the community."

With that, Ken opened the car door and settled himself in the driver's seat. As he started the car, he rolled down the window for a final word.

"Remember, David," he said, slowly backing out of the parking space, "everything starts with the gospel! Go find the soul and purpose of Midland Church. That's where you'll also find hope."

He gave a final wave and was gone.

CHAPTER 4

A Forgotten Document

It had been three days since the interesting man from Dallas had swept in and shaken up David's view of ministry, and now David found himself extremely frustrated.

"I almost wish Ken hadn't even come!" he confessed to his wife. "I have absolutely no idea what to do!"

Catherine sat on the living room couch with a blanket drawn over her legs. She watched David silently for a few moments as he stacked some small logs into their living room fireplace, and then said, "I don't understand. You were so happy on Saturday when you came home from meeting with him."

"Yes, I know," David said on a sigh, "but that was because he showed me what our church is missing."

"That we're not connected to the community?" Catherine ventured.

"Exactly. I've sensed it ever since we got here, but I wasn't able to put my finger on it, and that's why I was so excited when I talked with Ken and finally realized what the problem was." As David spoke, he began wadding up small pieces of newspaper and stuffing them between the bigger logs.

"But if he helped you see the problems with our church," Catherine said, "why is that a bad thing?"

"Because our church doesn't want to be connected to the community," David replied, the words coming in an impatient rush.

"What makes you say that?"

"Hello-o-o! Have you been here the past few months?" David violently crumpled up wads of paper. "The people here are very comfortable with the way things are, and they *do not want any change!*" As he spoke the last few words, he punctuated each one by jamming a wad of paper into the fireplace.

"Do you remember," David said, "when I tried to get the Board to advertise in the newspaper?" He walked to the utility closet.

"No," Catherine replied in a quiet voice.

"They absolutely refused to do it!" David rummaged through one of the plastic bins in the closet. "It would've cost $10 a month, but they wouldn't hear of it. Why, Fred Turner acted as if I were proposing to build a whole new wing on the church!" He finally found the lighter fluid he had been searching for and carried it back to the fireplace.

"The simple fact is," David continued, "I am not the senior pastor of Midland Church. I'm the senior pastor of the Midland Fellowship Club, and that's all I'm ever going to be!" As he spoke, he grew more agitated and squeezed the lighter fluid bottle onto the logs several times.

"That doesn't sound like my husband," Catherine said even more quietly. If David had really been listening to her, he would have heard the hurt and disappointment in her voice.

"Well, guess what?" he said, striking a match, "Welcome to the real . . . WHOA!!!" As soon as the match hit the fluid-soaked log, a ball of flame exploded out of the fireplace with a loud WHOOOOOMP! David was knocked back on his hands into a clumsy crab-walking position and remained that way for several seconds, blinking in confusion.

"Are you okay?" Catherine cried, leaning forward to jump up. But David was already cautiously getting to his feet.

"I'm fine," he said, looking over at his wife and truly seeing her for the first time since they had begun this conversation. He recognized the hurt and disappointment in her eyes and the defensive way she had curled into the end of the couch.

"Oh, Cath," he said as he walked over to her and sat down, "I'm so sorry." He put his arm around her and felt relief when she rested her head on his shoulder. "I'm not acting like myself tonight, am I?" he said.

Catherine said nothing but responded by giving his arm a squeeze.

"Things are gonna be okay," he said, more to himself than to her. "I just need to get my heart in the right place before anything else." They sat in silence for several minutes before Catherine spoke up again.

"Didn't Ken give you any advice?" she asked.

"Not much to speak of. He said that everything starts with the gospel, and that the only way we can keep our church off its inevitable death bed is to get back to the original purpose."

"Do you know what the original purpose of the church was?" Catherine asked.

David stood up and began to pace back and forth in front of the couch.

"I know that Midland Church was born about 40 years ago," he said, "and that the founding pastor was a man named Daniel Newcomb. But that's about all I know."

"What about talking to him?" Catherine suggested.

David stopped in front of her and tilted his head in consideration for a few seconds.

"I don't know anything about him," he mumbled sheepishly. "I don't even know if he's alive or dead." Hearing this, his wife stood up and kissed him on the cheek.

"Maybe you should find out," she said. With that, she walked down the hallway to their bedroom. After a few moments of standing alone in the middle of the room with his hands in his pockets, David decided that she might be right.

　　　　　　　　　　　❦

The next morning, as he entered the church, David felt a peculiar expectation well up inside his heart. He decided to skip his normal routine of writing e-mails and deleting spam, and headed straight for the storage room where the church archives were kept. He opened up a rusty folding chair and sat down in front of several large gray filing cabinets.

The room was dark and smelled musty, like an old basement. David sneezed twice as he opened up the first drawer.

"Open Sesame and God bless you," he said to himself as he began rifling through the papers inside. Unfortunately, the drawer was filled with hymn sheets, Sunday School attendance records, and not much else. David moved on to the second drawer, but all he found were gobs of yellow paper detailing committee reports and official meeting minutes.

"Third time's the charm," he said pulling out the last drawer. At first he was disappointed again; but then in the very back he spotted a large tan file labeled "Daniel Newcomb." David carefully lifted it out of its track and opened the file on his lap. At the very top was a leather folder marked "Church Constitution." David thought back to the church business class he and Catherine had taken together in Bible college. He remembered that all churches were required by law to draw up a constitution in order to establish the organization's structure, leadership, function and purpose.

"Wow . . . purpose," David mused aloud. Convinced that he had found something of value, David closed the last drawer of the filing cabinet and quickly walked back to his office. He leaned back in his chair, put his feet up on the desk, and began to read the original church constitution.

The first line got right to the point.

Article One—
The name of this church shall be: Midland Church.

Article Two almost took David's breath away.

Article Two—The purpose of this church:

- *Serve God through corporate worship.* As a gathering of believers, we endeavor to lift up the Lord Jesus Christ in our public worship. Our love for Him will be seen in the excellence of our music, prayers and proclamation of biblical truth. Midland Church will be a worshiping church.
- *Evangelize our community and the world.* It is the outpouring of our love for the Lord Himself that compels us to obey the Great Commission to take the gospel of Jesus Christ to the world. We will be continually mindful of the Lord's calling to love and reach out to those outside the household of faith with the good news of the gospel. Midland Church will be an evangelizing church.
- *Transform followers of Jesus Christ into fruit-bearing*

disciples. New believers will be given every opportunity to grow in the grace and knowledge of Jesus Christ in order to become fully mature in faith and witness. Midland Church will be a disciple-making church.

- *Care for the needs of each other.* We will serve one another as the highest expression of our service to the Lord Jesus Christ. Our service will meet the spiritual, physical and emotional needs of one another. Midland Church will be a caring church.

- *Serve our community through acts of service.* We will strive to provide a measure of Christ's compassion by serving the many needs of the people of Midland Church. This will include active community participation. Midland Church will be a compassionate, serving church.

David looked at the words in amazement. Here, in black and white, was everything he wanted so desperately to do with the church. Here was a vision of true ministry!

This is why God brought me here, he said to himself, feeling excitement and nervousness at the same time. *This stuff is right on target.* He looked up toward heaven and shouted, "Thank you, Jesus!" then turned his attention back to the purpose statement and was immediately struck by two things.

The first was the authority of Pastor Newcomb's words and the way he had emphasized the final sentence of each paragraph.

"Midland Church *will be*," David read aloud, "worshiping, evangelizing, disciple-making and serving." As he spoke these words, he was amazed at how far away the church had moved from its original purpose. What could have happened to push everything so far off course?

The second thing that struck him was the prevalence of the gospel. The entire reason the church had been born was to raise up a community of worshipers and then help them grow in love and respect for Jesus Christ. As David pondered this, he was immediately reminded of Ken Siever's words while Ken was backing his rental car away from the curb: "Everything starts with the gospel!" Ken had shouted.

Ken was right.

"He was right about everything," David whispered.

Dazed by the sheer number of thoughts and ideas that bombarded his mind, David stood up and began to pace back and forth in front of his desk. Gone was the frustration of last night. Gone was the sense of hopelessness. Now he was a divinely appointed man with a mission, and he intended to carry it out.

But how? He unconciously pinched the skin under

his chin as he pondered this question. There were several members of the congregation, like Ralph Nicholson and his wife, who had been around when Pastor Newcomb founded the church. David believed they would favor the words of this forgotten document and would be willing to return to its teaching. But then again, they were part of the group that had allowed the church to get off its original track. Were they aware of the disparity between the founding mission statement and the present life of the church, and could they be convinced to change?

David knew that fearfulness of what others might say and do would not help him find any answers, and so he decided to go to the source that was always helpful: He prayed—long and hard. He thanked the Lord for Midland Church and for the opportunity to shepherd God's people. He thanked the Lord for the members of the congregation, for the deacons and elders. He confessed his sins and the sins of the present church, and the sins of those who had gone before them. And then he prayed for wisdom, without which he wouldn't stand a chance with those he had come to serve.

Finally, after a long time on his knees, David stopped talking to God and began listening. And then, ever so slowly, a plan began to evolve in the back of his mind. It was a bold plan and even a little dangerous. But right away, David knew it was the right thing to do.

CHAPTER 5

The Awakening

The deacons and the elders of Midland Church met in the afternoon on the first Sunday of each month to discuss the issues and business of the church. That meant that David now had less than a week to perfect his plan. His first step, as always, was prayer—and he and Catherine committed to pray each day about the situation. They asked God to grant wisdom to the church and to the church leaders, along with receptive ears to hear.

David also spent as much time as he possibly could studying Scripture. He wanted to have an answer ready for any question that might come his way, and his favorite answers were always rooted solidly in the Bible. Once again, as David studied the New Testament

Church, he was amazed at how far Midland Church had moved from the biblical model.

"The original church leaders considered themselves the arms and legs of Jesus!" he told Catherine on Saturday as they prepared for Sunday's meeting. "I'm afraid I've been acting like a cushion rather than a bridge between the Lord and His people."

"We all have a lot to learn," Catherine replied, patting him on the arm. She pulled some papers out of the copy machine and handed them to David. "I know the Lord will be honored tomorrow," she said.

"Thank you, sweetheart," David replied as he glanced at the papers. "The Lord certainly has my attention!"

The next afternoon, the elders and deacons lazily made their way into the conference room. David had arrived early to greet each of the men as they arrived. He was feeling nervous and excited at the same time.

"Help me, Lord," he whispered for the umpteenth time that day. He smiled as he saw Ralph Nicholson walk through the door.

"Wonderful sermon, Pastor David," Ralph said, engulfing David's hand in his own and giving it a hearty shake. "Spoke to my heart."

"Why, thank you, Ralph," David replied, genuinely pleased.

The meeting was set to begin at 3:00 P.M. David glanced around the room to make sure everyone was present and accounted for. But when he looked toward the chair where Fred Turner usually sat, it was empty.

As David pondered this, he found himself unable to decide whether it was a blessing or a curse. On the one hand, out of all of the men seated around the conference table, Fred surely would have been the most vehemently opposed to David's new ideas. Fred had made it abundantly clear that he was happy with the church the way it was. At best, he was only lukewarm toward any kind of outreach into the community.

On the other hand, Fred was an integral part of the church leadership, and David had invested a lot of time in him during the past couple of months. David had taught with Fred and prayed with Fred and worked with Fred in an effort to build a meaningful relationship with this church leader. His efforts were finally producing results. David had noticed even within the past couple of weeks that Fred was letting his guard down more and more. So David had no desire to implement a plan in Fred's absence. But without Fred here today, he didn't have a choice.

However, before Ralph called the meeting to order, the door burst open and Fred wobbled in, panting.

"Sorry, folks!" he gasped, out of breath. "I decided to walk on account of the warm weather, but I s'pose I'm a sight slower than I used to be!" Before taking a seat at the table he made his way to David.

"Good to see ya, Pastor," he said, offering his hand. David clasped Fred's hand and smiled.

I hope this isn't our last handshake, David thought to himself, and then watched Fred walk to the back of the room and sit down.

David signaled to Ralph Nicholson to open the meeting with prayer. Then several of the elders and deacons reviewed the decisions that had been made at the last meeting and reported on the various consequences and outcomes of actions taken. When they were finished with their reports, Ralph stood up and announced that it was time to discuss new items of business. He looked over at David.

"Our Pastor has been workin' very hard on a presentation he'd like all of us to hear. You have the floor now, Pastor David." Ralph sat down, and David walked toward the whiteboard.

"We had a very interesting guest come to our church a couple of weeks ago," David began, smiling slightly as he pictured Ken Siever in his dusty jeans and white cowboy hat. "He came from a company called Ministry Solutions, in Dallas, and he opened my eyes to a lot of things about our church that I think all of you should know." David paused for several seconds in order to build up a little suspense. As he glanced around the room, he spotted Fred Turner, whose expression showed that he was both wary and curious.

"Before we get into all that, I have asked Terry Sullivan to give us the annual attendance report."

Terry had been recently appointed as a deacon and was one of the youngest men in the group, which was why David had chosen him for this moment.

"So far this year," Terry began, reading mechanically from a sheet of paper, "we have added three new members to our church. We have also had five members leave the church. Four moved away, and one is no longer attending, due to a conflict of interest."

Terry started to sit down when David said, "Terry, in your research of our church attendance, how does this year's report compare to our history?"

Terry, who had started to sit down, remained frozen in a half squat for a few seconds and then straightened up.

"Ummm," he began, "it seems pretty consistent with our attendance patterns over the last decade or so."

"Would you elaborate, please?" David said. Terry had prepared well in advance with Pastor David and was ready with an answer.

"Well, it seems that every year we pretty much gain as many people as we lose."

"I see," David said, tapping the table as if he were mentally crunching the numbers. "Does anyone here know the technical term for when a church's attendance stays pretty much the same over a span of years?" He looked around the room as he spoke to see if anyone would venture a guess.

When no one spoke, David said, "It's called flat-lining."

As Fred Turner listened to David speak, his alarm and unease increased and began to show on his face. He was an intelligent man, and he could see where David was going with all of his talk about attendance and growth. Fred blurted the first wisecrack that came to mind.

"Flatlining," he said, looking around at his fellow deacons for support "Well, that sounds about as serious as a heart attack!" Several of the men sitting close to Fred laughed.

David put his hands on the back of his chair and leaned over the table in Fred's direction.

"Do any of you think a flatlining church is in serious trouble?" he asked.

"Sure don't!" Fred quipped. "We faithfully worship and serve God here at Midland Church while the world continues to move further away from God."

Silence reigned in the conference room. The elders and deacons had not expected their cheerful young pastor to speak so gravely about church attendance, and none of them knew quite what to say. After another long pause, David's face brightened.

"Don't worry," he said cheerfully, "Jesus was once dead, and He rose triumphantly from the grave!" This comment accomplished little in lightening the heaviness in the room. As David looked into their eyes, he saw the precise combination of confusion and curiosity that he had been aiming for, and he decided to reveal the rest of his plan.

"Would you like to hear what Ken Siever, a church consultant from Dallas, said about our church?" Most of the men mumbled affirmative answers while the rest shook their heads.

"Ken said that we're no longer fulfilling our purpose."

The atmosphere erupted in a babble of comments as the elders and deacons attempted to interpret Ken Siever's criticism. David had spent the past few days planning how to get this kind of reaction—it was important for the leaders to first react emotionally to Ken's words. If all went according to plan, the present discussion would prepare them for Dr. Newcomb's purpose statements from the original church constitution.

It was Fred Turner who first took the bait.

"Now hold on a minute!" he said. He stood up, his hand shaking as he pointed a finger at David and said, "How in the world does this friend of yours even know what the purpose of this church is, or was, or is going to be? He doesn't know a lick about us, and I'm not so sure that you do either!"

Click! David could almost hear the hinges of his

"trap" spring shut as Fred stepped into it. David quickly sprang into action.

"I don't mean to upset you, Fred," David said as he scooped up a small stack of papers sitting in front of him, "but I do believe the answer to your question is found in these papers."

Before Fred could say anything else, David flew around the table and handed a copy of Dr. Newcomb's original purpose statement to each of the elders and deacons. For most of the men, this was the first time they had encountered the document; however, a few of the men had seen it before, and their faces took on the dreamy look of fond memories from the distant past.

"I haven't seen this in 10 years!" quipped one of the elders.

"I thought we only got these out for church fights!" another said in a joking tone. Soon all of the men were hunched over the table, busily reading and discussing the original words of Dr. Newcomb. As David watched, he began to think that his plan just might work after all.

Suddenly, Fred Turner's angry voice blurted, "What does this document have to do with Ken Siever's criticism of our church? Church constitutions are just paperwork required by the government!"

Several of the men (especially those sitting close to Fred) began to disagree. Few were buying Fred's line.

Most realized this document was more than mere legal script required by the IRS.

Ralph Nicholson stepped in to save the day.

"Wait a minute, Fred," the big man broke in, speaking slowly but forcefully. "My wife and I were foundin' members of this church, and we were here when Dr. Newcomb wrote up this constitution. He pulled it right outta the Bible, with Scripture verses backin' up everything he said. So I suggest you listen up and let Pastor David say what he wants to say."

Fred looked abashed and slumped back in his chair with an angry "Harumph!" All eyes were back on David to find out what he would say next.

"Thank you, Ralph," David said, genuinely grateful for Ralph's intervention. And then an idea popped into his mind. "Ralph," he said, with a peculiar smile on his face, "since you were here when this document was written, would you mind reading the purpose statement to us?"

The big man scratched the back of his head before answering.

"Well, I suppose not," he said, and then began to read.

What followed could later only be understood as an important spiritual moment in the lives of the men in that room. Ralph's voice, with its Southern accent, was powerful and melodic as he slowly read and emphasized the final sentence of each paragraph with an authority that seemed to come from heaven itself. When he finished, a quiet breeze ruffled through the conference room from the open door. Several of the loose sheets of paper lying on the table scattered, but no one seemed to notice.

The change in the room's atmosphere was visceral, and David could see on the men's faces that they now believed what he had so recently discovered.

"I think we all realize," David said, "that the church we're leading today is very different from the one that Dr. Newcomb founded." Most of the men nodded, some of them as if they were still hypnotized by Ralph's voice.

"Not only that," David said, "but I think we need to consider that the church we are leading today has lost its way. Thank you, Ralph, for reading the purpose of Midland Church. Those words came from the heart of our founder, Dr. Newcomb. They are biblically based and they should be taken quite seriously. Given the chance, those beautiful words may come alive in our hearts once again."

Fred Turner could not believe his ears; but he was no one's fool. He realized he had lost whatever momentum he may have had, and this was David's hour. He decided to zip his mouth or incur the wrath of the others.

Tears welled in Ralph's eyes, and an unstoppable tide of emotion filled the room as good men confirmed the words that Ralph had so eloquently read.

Gathering his composure, Ralph said, "So what do we do now, Pastor David?" Unfortunately, David had no answer to give him. He had spent so much time planning how to get the church leaders to see this vital document that he had forgotten to figure out the next step! To be honest, David could hardly believe the Lord had moved these men so far so fast.

"Well, Ralph . . ." David said, then paused as he sent up a prayer for wisdom. And then the next step came to his mind like a divine birthday present.

"I think we should pray!" David declared. And that is exactly what happened. For the next hour, each man got down on his knees and poured out his heart to God. Some of the men confessed that the church had been taken over by their own selfish desires, and they begged forgiveness of the Lord for leading the congregation in the wrong direction. Others thanked the Lord for the gift of Midland Church and for the new chance to reach out to the community.

Through it all, each man's heart began to swell with God's peace and a sense of unity as he experienced the confirming power of the Holy Spirit. Each man, that is, except for one.

As the time of prayer concluded, David looked at his watch and realized they were almost late for the evening service. He quickly called for a vote to adjourn the meeting, which was immediately seconded and passed. The group decided to hold an emergency meeting the following week after church in order to start the process of getting everything back on track. As the men began to exit the room, David challenged them to brainstorm possible solutions and ideas before they met again.

Inside the sanctuary, an excited buzz began to circulate throughout the congregation as the deacons and elders joined their families for the evening service. It seemed that everyone could tell right away that something important had just happened, and David decided to capitalize on the excitement.

"Ladies and gentlemen," he began, standing behind the podium. He glanced at Catherine in the front row and gave her a wink and a quick thumbs-up, then continued speaking. "As you can probably tell, the church leaders and I have just concluded a meeting that I barely have words to describe. The Lord poured out his blessings and grace on us, and we have some very important things to tell you in regard to the future of our church. However, we're going to need a few weeks to get ourselves organized and form a plan of action. For now, I'm just going to ask you to trust us and to be patient, and to pray for the Lord's will for Midland Church."

These words elicited a favorable response from the congregation as the people turned to each other to discuss what he could possibly mean. David waited for the noise to die down, and then delivered his prepared remarks as if nothing unusual had happened at all. But he could hardly contain himself.

When the service ended, several people tried to get him to spill the beans, but he and the other church leaders were resolute and refused to budge. "Please trust us and give us a little time," was the consistent answer from the leaders.

"You'll know in a few weeks," was their mantra, along with, "Please remember to pray." After a fair amount of time had passed, the sanctuary emptied of people, and David found himself alone with his wife for what seemed like the first time in ages.

"It went well, Cath," he said, exhausted but smiling brightly. "I can't wait to tell you about it!"

"And I can't wait to hear!" she replied, kissing him on the cheek. "I'm going to go home and get dinner started. I'll see you in a few minutes?"

"Yep," he replied, rubbing his stomach, "I'll bring my appetite, that's for sure!" After his wife left, David finished putting away the sound equipment and walked down the hall toward his office. He was locking the door before going home when he heard a cold, flinty voice say, "I know what this is all about." David turned around and saw Fred Turner leaning casually against the church mailboxes.

"What do you mean, Fred?"

"I mean, I know why you're here." Fred pushed off from the wall and walked a few steps closer to the main office door. On the outside he appeared calm and collected—even polite. But as he walked past one of the outside windows a beam of light passed over his face, and David saw that Fred's expression was set like stone.

"I'm here because this is where God called me and my family," David replied, feeling the need to make some kind of stand.

"Uh huh," Fred said, nodding his head slowly up and down, "and pretty soon the Big Man Upstairs'll call you to take out a loan and build a fancy new addition to the sanctuary for all the crowds you're gonna preach to." As he spoke, Fred's gaze moved past David to the wall behind him, almost as if the older man were watching some kind of slide show of his past life.

"And then," he continued, "those big crowds won't show up, but the loan officers will, won't they. They'll come knockin' all right, and then you'll stand up one Sunday and announce that God is callin' you somewhere else after all, and then you'll take your family and your big dreams and leave town and never come back." He remained calm as he spoke, but his eyes watched the scenes play out on the wall behind David, and every now and then he would flinch as if physically struck.

"Is that what happened to you?" David asked,

beginning to understand some of the motivation behind Fred's continued antagonism toward evangelism. The question seemed to awaken the older man out of whatever memory he had been reliving, and his eyes once again focused on the pastor.

"Never you mind," Fred replied, reaching into his pocket. For a brief moment an image flashed through David's mind of Fred pulling out a weapon, but it turned out to be only car keys.

"I just want you to know," Fred said, jingling his keys until he had singled out the appropriate one, "that I'm on to you, and that I ain't gonna just sit back and let you destroy my church." He paused and looked questioningly at David, as if waiting for a response. "Nothin' to say for yourself?" he asked, allowing a little bit of sarcasm to flavor his tone of voice.

David remained silent. He was wise enough to see that Fred was fishing for a fight and decided to heed the advice from Proverbs concerning a fool and his mouth.

"I guess that's just as well," Fred said eventually, although he looked disappointed. "Just as long as you and I understand one another." With that, Fred gave his key ring one more shake and then walked out the door and into the night. After a few deep breaths, David followed, and went home.

CHAPTER 6

The Original Vision

Of all the earthly things Dr. Daniel Newcomb loved, he loved his wife the best. Second place on that list, however, belonged to lemonade. Throughout his entire life, Dr. Newcomb had been absolutely enthralled with lemonade. He drank it with his toast and eggs at breakfast; he sipped it with his salads at lunch; and he positively guzzled it on the porch after dinner. In fact, he was so infatuated with the drink that he used to pour a little bit into the sink each day before he prayed, as if he were making an offering of it to God.

And so it was that two days after the revelatory meeting of the elders and deacons, David and Catherine found themselves sitting in the living room of a quaint old house in the middle of the country—drinking lemonade.

"This is wonderful!" David said after taking a sip.

"Well, thank you," replied Dr. Newcomb, sending a quick wink toward his wife. "Mary makes it for me every now and then, and I think it's pretty good."

The older man took another gulp, relishing its sweet tartness, and studied the visiting couple in silence for a few moments. He was intrigued by the two of them and had been ever since they had knocked on his door almost an hour ago. He and his wife had often wondered how things were going back in the little church they had founded almost 40 years previously. As he continued to study the younger man and sipped his favorite lemonade in his favorite chair, he felt as if a prayer had been answered.

"As I was telling you," David said, "there are a lot of interesting things going on back in Midland." With a clear voice and a calm spirit, he relayed to the aging couple the recent adventures of Midland Church, beginning with their Sunday call after the potluck to shepherd the church, and ending with the energetic evening service a couple of nights before.

David felt a great relief to tell the elder pastor about his plunge into the role of senior pastor of Midland and about the feeling of something wrong that had continually plagued him almost since the beginning. He spoke of Ken Siever, and of the sickness that Ken had exposed. And he spoke of the meeting with the deacons and elders and of the Lord's powerful presence that had shaken them all as they prayed. The only thing David did not speak of was his encounter with Fred Turner. That event he had relayed to Catherine alone and had charged her to not speak of it with anyone else.

"Well, my land!" exclaimed Dr. Newcomb when the younger man stopped speaking. He glanced sideways at his wife, who was sitting next to him, holding his hand. "Sounds like the Spirit's at work once again," he said to his wife, squeezing her hand.

David and Catherine were enjoying seeing this couple who were almost in their eighties still enjoying holding hands!

They're just like us, David mused.

"Do you know what happened to the church?" David asked carefully, addressing Dr. Newcomb. "Do you know when things started to change?"

The old man sighed heavily and glanced at his wife before answering.

"It's not something that happened in a day," he finally said. "When Mary and I retired 14 years ago—"

"Fifteen, dear," Mary interjected.

"Fifteen? Really?" Dr. Newcomb glanced at his wife and winked.

"Fifteen, Daniel, I'm sure of it." She had a mischievous glint in her eye that David found fascinating.

"Anyway," continued Dr. Newcomb, "when we left 15 years ago, the ministry was healthy and the church reached out to the people of Midland in a number of ways." His voice sounded wistful, and he looked up at the ceiling as he spoke.

"When I retired, we made it a point to move back to our original home here in Shady Grove. This is where the Lord called us to ministry. Well, I really didn't want the next pastor to feel like I was looking over his shoulder."

David took a sip of lemonade and casually smiled to affirm the wisdom of the older man's decision.

"However," Dr. Newcomb continued, "Mary and I have always had friends back in Midland, and so we've heard things from time to time. I know that they went through several pastors in about 10 years, which I'm sure was very stressful."

"That seems to be a typical reaction after a founding pastor leaves," David said when the older man paused to gather his thoughts.

"Yes," replied Dr. Newcomb, "unfortunately it is. Anyway, I think that in the midst of all the turmoil the church forgot about my original vision and just wanted to settle. I think the leaders began to focus more on stability than on making a difference for God. Do you see what I mean?"

David nodded. "That certainly makes sense," he said, "and that certainly fits with what I've encountered there since we arrived."

"Yep," Dr. Newcomb replied. "It's unfortunate. Sometimes Mary and I feel like we should go back and try to help them fix things. But we're old—Ouch!"

David and Catherine caught the slight movement of Mary's fingers as she pinched her husband's arm.

"Okay, okay," chuckled Dr. Newcomb. "*I'm* old— almost 80. But Mary here is still a spring chicken! Anyway, we were at peace that God had closed that chapter of our lives; but we're thrilled to see that He has called you and your lovely wife to step in. Do you have any kind of plan set up?"

"Actually," David said with some fervor, "that's exactly what we came here to talk about." He signaled to Catherine as he spoke, and she pulled a weather-beaten leather folder out of the side pocket of her purse and handed it to her husband.

"I think this should be familiar to you," David said.

"Oh, my!" the older man shouted, carefully taking the leather folder in his hands as if it were a delicate flower or a helpless little child. He slowly leafed through the document, pausing on each page.

"The personal notes written in the margins are still readable," David said as he watched the old man. "Are they yours?"

Dr. Newcomb smiled and looked up. His face seemed younger as he said, "It's like I've found an old friend."

"Will you tell us about it?" David asked, leaning forward earnestly and directing his question at both Dr. Newcomb and his wife. "Will you tell us how it all started?"

The elder couple looked at one another with dreamy eyes and then settled back in their chairs as if preparing for a very long drive. At length Dr. Newcomb cleared his throat, and after energizing himself with several gulps of his favorite beverage, he began their story.

"It all started with my original vision. When I received it, I was a young man working as an associate pastor. Is something wrong?" he asked, suddenly noticing the puzzled look on David's face.

"I'm sorry," David said, blushing slightly, "You've used the term 'original vision' but I'm not really familiar with what you mean by it."

The older man pondered for a few moments and then said, "An 'original vision' occurs when God moves the heart of one of his own and deeply impresses him to take a decisive step of faith. Kind of like Abraham being led to leave Ur and head somewhere far away that he knew nothing about."

"Are you talking about vision in the context of

divine revelation, like the Scriptures?" David asked.

"Heavens no," replied Dr. Newcomb, shaking his head, "nothing so divine as that. Remember that the book of Revelation tells us that anyone who attempts to add to the Scriptures is cursed with a curse!"

David got the point, visibly relieved.

"No," continued Dr. Newcomb, changing his course, "I use the term 'original vision' to describe an intense desire or compulsion to do something for the Lord. It's like a volcano inside of you that explodes with the energy and potential to accomplish something very special for God. By the way, did God speak to you in an audible voice in the middle of the night and tell you to go to Midland?"

"No, He didn't," David said. "He did just as you have described. A deep desire rose up in me to go serve when the opportunity came."

At this, Dr. Newcomb raised his eyebrows in recognition, and the young pastor nodded his head, urging the old man to continue.

"My original vision," said Dr. Newcomb, "was for the town of Midland. The Lord revealed it to my heart as a ripe field much in need of harvesting. I remember another picture that came to my mind back then. It was a picture of a lighthouse standing boldly against fierce and oppressive elements!" As he spoke, Dr. Newcomb involuntarily laid his right hand upon his chest, as if he were once again pledging allegiance to that glorious cause. Suddenly, he lowered his hand and looked pointedly at David.

"Does that sound at all familiar, Pastor Newman?" he asked.

David laughed. "Well, in that context, I've been given a vision too," he replied. "After my first sermon at Midland, I was walking to my car in the parking lot when I looked back at the church and for just a moment I pictured in my mind a storm just like you described."

"Really!" declared Dr. Newcomb. "What did you see?"

"Well, instead of a dilapidated old church building, I saw a lighthouse, and it was shining the light of the gospel out to the whole community around it—warning of danger, and at the same time, bringing people to safety."

Dr. Newcomb closed his eyes with pleasure and smiled grandly.

"Yeeessssssss," he sighed, leaning back in his chair.

"But, I'm afraid at this point our little lighthouse is broken," David said, "and it isn't doing much good to anybody except to the few who are inside."

Mary Newcomb nodded earnestly at this comment.

"The people there all have good hearts," she said, "but they are also easily distracted."

"They need a shepherd," Dr. Newcomb added.

"Or a lighthouse-keeper," interposed David thoughtfully. After a brief period of silence, Dr. Newcomb continued with his story.

"Yes, it was a vision as obvious to me as if God had come down and scribbled it on my heart. Of course," he said with a wry smile, "there were obstacles."

"It's true," Mary said, smiling at her husband. "At first I wanted no part of it. The town was unsightly and dull compared to where I grew up, and it seemed to me like an enormous waste of Daniel's time—and talents." She playfully tweaked her husband's ear as she said this.

"But," she continued, still smiling, "he was very persistent, and in the end his steadfast confidence that God was calling us there rubbed off on me."

When Mary had finished speaking of those early years, a smile found its way to Catherine's lips, and she looked into her own husband's eyes.

"I know what you mean, Mary," she said. "It all seemed hard and strange to me at first, but I trusted David, and I knew that he was following the Lord."

"Anyway," Dr. Newcomb said, "when we arrived, we knew what we had to do, and we did it with all of our being—heart, soul, mind and strength! The first couple we met . . ."

In the next hour and a half, Dr. and Mrs. Newcomb

entertained their guests with anecdotes and stories from a time gone by. As David listened, he became more and more certain that his and Catherine's own situation was a continuation of the work the Newcombs had begun.

It was an important work, David knew, and the Lord was with them. But still, as he listened, a conviction came upon him that it was possible for him to fail, and that there would be dire consequences for the entire town if he did.

───※───

I will not fail, David said to himself later as he walked with his wife down the Newcombs's driveway to the car. In his mind was the burning image of a tall lighthouse flashing in the darkness, illuminating the crags and rocks around the shore and steering a fleet of ships away from certain disaster.

CHAPTER 7

The Five *R*s

On the following Sunday, David once again stood at the entrance to the conference room greeting the deacons and elders as they filed in and sat down around the table. The attitude in the room was vastly different from what it had been only a week ago. There was very little socializing among the group, and most of the men seemed fidgety, as if they were overflowing with a nervous energy unfamiliar to them.

When the last deacon had sat down, David nodded to Ralph, who cleared his throat before standing up.

"Pastor asked me to start things off with a little devotion," Ralph announced. "So here goes." He picked up his large leather Bible and flipped to the beginning. "I'm gonna be readin' from Genesis chapter 11."

Several of the men opened their own Bibles at this announcement, while others murmured in surprise.

David himself was surprised. Genesis 11 was the story of the Tower of Babel—a strange passage to begin such an important meeting. Still, David had seen his big friend come through for him on several occasions, and decided to trust him.

"Now the whole earth had one language and the same words," Ralph began. Just as he had the week before, he read with a clear, patient voice that contained a gentle authority that almost hypnotized the group. He seemed to emphasize verse 6: "And the Lord said, 'Behold, they are one people, and they have all one language, and this is only the beginning of what they will do. And nothing that they propose to do will now be impossible for them.'"

When he finished reading through verse 8, he gently laid his Bible on the table and looked around the room at his friends. He took special care to meet the eyes of Fred Turner, who was sitting in the far left corner and seemed disinterested in the whole affair. Shaking his head slightly, Ralph addressed the group.

"I've been studyin' on these verses for a little while now, and I think there's a couple of things that are important for us to know and believe before we go any further." Several of the men nodded their heads in consent, and Ralph nodded his own in return.

"First of all, it's pretty clear these folks were in rebellion against God; but I don't think that was the only reason He decided to come down here and deal with them."

Several of the men shook their heads to show they didn't think so either, and Ralph responded with a quick shake of his own.

"It seems to me that God came down because them folks had found the secret to success but were using it to accomplish the wrong things." After a brief pause, Ralph picked up his Bible once again and reread the second half of verse 6: "And nothing that they propose to do will now be impossible for them."

"It also seems to me," Ralph said, "that their secret to success had three parts: they all had the same goal; they all had the same language; they all worked together." Ralph looked around the room expectantly. After a few moments, one of the men gravely nodded his head, and Ralph nodded his gravely in return.

"So then I said to myself, If these three things was forceful enough to get God's attention for somethin' bad, why can't we use 'em for somethin' good?

"In other words, I think we can use the keys to success to help our own church now that we know we've gotten a might off track." He clasped his hands in front of him and cracked his knuckles as if preparing to get serious.

"Most of us here only speak one language," Ralph said, "so there ain't no problem there. And I don't think we've had any problems workin' together over the years. So it seems to me that our trouble lies with our goals."

"Wait a minute there, Ralph," Fred said. He had become more and more agitated as he listened to the big man speak. "Are you sayin' we've had different goals when it comes to leadin' this church?"

"No sir, Fred, I'm not sayin' that," Ralph replied.

"Then what's the problem?"

"The problem, as I see it," Ralph said slowly, "is that we've got ourselves a bad goal—just like them Babblers did." A few of the younger deacons chuckled at Ralph's choice of words; but when they saw his earnest and concerned expression, their laughter stopped abruptly.

Ralph spoke slowly and mournfully. "The Bible says that those folks decided to build themselves a tower because they wanted to make a name for themselves, instead of wantin' to do their work for God's glory.

"I think we've built ourselves this here church because we want to be comfortable; and I don't think we've been bringin' God the glory any more than them Babblers did all those years ago."

There was no nodding or shaking of heads from the rest of the group this time—their faces had become like Ralph's, and they were considering his words.

"I guess what I'm sayin'," Ralph concluded, "is that

we've been usin' the keys to success for the wrong reasons, and I think we need to turn it around now before God comes down and scatters us away." When he was finished speaking, he sat down and looked at David as if he were looking at the church's only hope.

"Terry, would you please pray for us as we start?" Pastor David said, meeting the eyes of the young deacon he had terrified at the last meeting. Fortunately, David had talked with Terry before the meeting, so the young man promptly stood and bowed his head, and the other men followed suit.

"Oh, Lord God," Terry prayed, "You are holy and worthy of praise. You are also worthy of a church that brings You glory and does the work that You have put us here to do." Several amens were voiced.

"Father, we know that the Great Commission tells us to go out into the community and save the lost for You, and we haven't been doing that. We confess our ignorance and our disobedience, Lord, and we ask Your forgiveness." Terry paused for a moment, and around the room there was the sound of similar whispered pleas for mercy.

"Lord," Terry continued, "We know that You are a God of second chances, and so we ask for a second chance as the leaders of this church. Please help us fix what's been broken, right what's been wronged, and find what's been lost. In Jesus' name, amen."

"Amen!!!" echoed the group. As they raised their heads and blinked themselves back into the light, they saw that Pastor David was now standing by the whiteboard and had drawn five large *R*s in a vertical column on the left side.

"Thank you, Terry," David said with a nod in the deacon's direction, and then his gaze included all of the men around the table.

"Gentlemen, we have some work to do—but I'm excited!" David quickly summarized his conversation with Dr. and Mrs. Newcomb.

"As you know," David said, "Dr. Newcomb had a plan for this church when it was founded. He called it an 'original vision.'" David drew a rough sketch of a field on the far right edge of the whiteboard, complete with tufts of grass and rolling hills in the background.

"Dr. Newcomb's vision was of the city of Midland as a field ripe with fruit and ready to be harvested. Interestingly, Dr. Newcomb and I both considered the purpose and function of Midland Church as a lighthouse. The only difference is that he thought of a lighthouse 40 years before I did." David pointed to his drawing. "So, when I talk about his original vision, I'm talking about his God-given goal for starting this church." He drew a rough sketch of a church building on the left side of the board, including a large steeple on the top.

"As you know," David said, "Dr. Newcomb was able to accomplish this goal, and he used this church to bring many people to Christ from the city of Midland—including some of you in this room today."

The elders and deacons nodded with warm smiles on their faces, many of them remembering their first visit to the church all those years ago.

David drew a line connecting the church with the picture of the field. "Dr. Newcomb was able to do this because he had a solid plan, and he stuck to it." As soon as David wrote the words "Church Constitution" on top of the connecting line, he held up the original document to emphasize his point.

"So last week we discovered that we've lost sight of Dr. Newcomb's original vision and that our church has forgotten its original purpose. It is our job today to figure out how to get ourselves back on track. Is everyone with me so far?"

The men around the table nodded agreement, and David turned back to the whiteboard with a different color marker in his hand. Underneath the line labeled "Church Constitution" he drew five vertical lines—each with a small rectangle attached to the top.

"During the past few days," David said, "I've come up with five steps—I call them signposts—that I think we need to take in order to get back to Dr. Newcomb's original vision. Can I share them with you?"

The men were impressed by David's simple approach, and encouraging words rang out around the table.

David filled in the first *R* of the vertical column on the left.

SIGNPOST #1:
REDISCOVER OUR PURPOSE

As David finished writing, he once again held up the old leather folder containing Dr. Newcomb's church constitution.

"In a lot of ways," he said, "I think our purpose has already been rediscovered. Don't you agree?" Several of the men around the table nodded their heads.

"Still, I think it'll do us good to prepare Dr. Newcomb's purpose statement for a presentation to the church. We need to be clear and accurate, but we also need to create headings that will stick to the congregation's minds and hearts."

As soon as he finished speaking, the brainstorming began. Most of the elders and deacons had brought their copies of the original purpose statement, and now they began discussing how to express each part of the statement in as few words as possible.

After about 10 minutes, it became clear to David that most of the men were partial to the last sentence in each of Dr. Newcomb's points. He suggested that those sentences form the backbone of the new communication piece, and everyone heartily agreed.

Thirty minutes later, they were finished, and Pastor David wrote the new headings in a box at the top righthand corner of the whiteboard.

We exist as a community of believers to:

- Worship God
- Evangelize our world
- Disciple believers
- Care for one another
- Serve our community

David took a step away from the board and examined the statement approvingly. "This is a great first step," he said, turning his eyes back toward the group. "From these headings we will direct the church to consider each of Dr. Newcomb's detailed purpose statements.

"I have one more thing to say about this *R*, and then we can move on. One of the reasons I visited with Dr. Newcomb was to get a better understanding of his original vision for this church. I learned that spreading the gospel was at the heart of everything he wanted to do. Therefore, I think—"

"One second, Pastor David—if you please." It was Fred Turner speaking. But this time his interruption came without any of the recent anger or vehemence he had shown. David turned around cautiously and was surprised to see a genuine smile on Fred's face.

"I'm still a little confused about this 'original vision' thing," the deacon said. "Do you mean that Pastor Newcomb's vision for the gospel still applies today, even though it's almost 40 years old?"

David's mind scanned through Fred's question and tone of voice in an attempt to locate any sarcasm or trickery, but there seemed to be nothing but the question itself.

"Well, yes, I do think it applies," David said, deciding to treat Fred's question as an honest one. "Dr. Newcomb's vision for Midland Church has everything to do with the gospel. He felt compelled to proclaim the saving grace of Jesus Christ. I can't imagine a church placing any greater purpose or priority above that of the gospel of Jesus Christ.

"Furthermore, the very message entrusted to us by the Lord Himself was never meant to be hidden or held back from this world that Jesus came to save. The gospel must once again become—and remain—our priority at Midland Church as long as the church continues to operate."

"Thank ya, Pastor," Fred said, still smiling, "I just

wanted to make sure I understood." He sat down and waited for David to continue speaking.

Maybe there's still hope for him, David thought to himself as he nodded toward Fred before walking back to the board.

"Fred's question brings us right to the second signpost," David said.

David wrote the words:

SIGNPOST #2:
RETURN TO THE ORIGINAL VISION

"This is where we are now," David said, after allowing the group to digest the words of the signpost for a few moments. "Our purpose as God's kingdom representatives is to connect with one another and at the same time connect with our community. That's just another way of saying that we need to be about our Father's business; and His business is getting the gospel out through us."

"How do we do that?" asked one of the elders.

"I'm glad you asked," said David. "But first let me make a distinction between purpose and vision. Our *purpose statement* is a description of our reason for existence. Moreover, it is a portrait of who we are and what we do.

"A *vision* is our destination. Identifying who we are makes it possible to understand where we're going. To do this, each of us needs to set aside the traditional magnifying glass most often used to scrutinize—and criticize—the church and replace it with a pair of binoculars. With binoculars we can all get a better glimpse of Midland Church 10 years from now."

"Do you mean that as church leaders we're to focus on the future?" asked a deacon sitting close to the board.

David nodded and said, "Better yet, we're to set a course of action and then hold it for as long as the Lord keeps us here. Setting our course affects where we are today and where we hope to be someday."

David scanned every man's expression and then said, "Does everyone agree that Dr. Newcomb's purpose statements should also be ours?"

The leaders affirmed his question without hesitation.

"Good! After reading through several of our founder's papers, and talking to him personally, I suggest we craft a vision statement together. Here are several key words we may want to include." David scratched out a quick list.

- Vision
- Gospel
- Midland Church
- Jesus Christ

- Community/World
- Reach/Impact

Within minutes the men had come up with a finely crafted statement now written across the whiteboard. The wordsmiths on the team argued for a few moments over the word "impact" and reached a compromise by replacing it with the words "greatly influence."

MIDLAND CHURCH'S VISION:
TO GREATLY INFLUENCE OUR COMMUNITY AND THE WORLD WITH THE LIFE-CHANGING GOSPEL OF JESUS CHRIST

"Now that's a big vision!" Ralph said with a whistle.

"Is it too big?" David asked, then quickly continued by saying, "It's hard to believe that such a statement could come together so quickly. You guys are simply outstanding."

Young Terry spoke up. "I just think the Lord is in this. And you know what? We have some serious work to do to fulfill this vision. I make a motion that we accept it before we get carried away with too much wordsmithing."

The motion was seconded, and within moments the vision of Midland Church found a permanent home.

Ralph interjected another thought. "If we've already gone to the trouble of revisitin' and summarizin' our church constitution, why don't we keep followin' that example?"

David's questioning look prompted the big man to explain.

"Well, I'm talkin' about followin' our U.S. Constitution. The folks that wrote it signed it to show they were serious. So why don't we all throw our own John Hancocks on this work we've done?"

"I think that's a great idea, Ralph!" David exclaimed, his face brightening.

Instructions were given to print out a copy of the headings, the original purpose statements, and the church vision while the group took a 10-minute break.

When the new document was passed around the table for each elder and deacon to sign, Ralph was given the privilege of the first signature. And just like Mr. Hancock, he proudly wrote his name in large script.

David watched intently as the sheet reached Fred Turner. It looked as if Fred wanted nothing to do with the paper, but he signed it anyway, with furrowed brow and a frown on his face.

David was the last to receive the vision statement, and he joyfully signed it, then held it up over his head to be affirmed by a warm round of applause from all of the elders and deacons—all except one. By this time, it was clear that Fred Turner had mentally checked out of the meeting and was no longer interested in visions or covenants, or anything of the sort.

So much for turning things around, David thought.

"All right!" he said aloud to the group. "This is another great step; but I think it's important to remember that we still need to help the rest of the church rediscover its purpose and return to God's vision. So that brings me to the third *R*!"

SIGNPOST #3:
REDEDICATE THE CHURCH FAMILY

"I think this is going to be fun!" said Pastor David. His cheerfulness spread around the table to the rest of the men. "But it's also going to take a lot of work."

One of the men rolled up his sleeves as a visual response to the Pastor's exhortation.

David nodded at him with a smile and said, "What we need to do is come up with a plan to present our new Covenant to the rest of the church body. Anyone have any ideas?"

The elders and deacons began a lively discussion about the methods and priorities of addressing the church body. As each man presented his thoughts, Pastor David kept a watchful eye on Terry Sullivan. David knew that Terry was a marketing manager for a large company in Midland, and he hoped the young deacon would take a leadership role in this phase of the plan. Thankfully, it didn't take long for David's hopes to come true.

"I have an idea," Terry said, jumping into the group conversation when there was an extended pause. "We need some kind of picture or image that will help us communicate the vision to the other members."

"Do you mean a logo?" asked one of the other deacons.

"Something like that," Terry said thoughtfully. "Something like a word picture that will help us organize our thoughts—maybe some kind of visual analogy that we could explain as part of our presentation."

"I think I know what you mean," broke in Ralph. "Maybe we could use Pastor Newcomb's idea of a lighthouse as part of his original vision." He looked at Pastor David before continuing. David began to understand what Ralph was saying and started to think about his own idea.

"That's exactly what I'm talking about, Ralph!" Terry said, "I know that Dr. Newcomb also envisioned a ripe field. But from a marketing point of view, a field may not be as thought-provoking as a lighthouse."

A farmer in the group confirmed this but added, "Well, a field sure represents a whole lotta work!"

"We ain't tryin' to put a commercial on TV," said another elder.

Terry looked abashed and was about to apologize when Pastor David broke in.

"I have an idea," he said, rubbing his chin thoughtfully. "Remember that Pastor Newcomb wasn't the only one who envisioned a lighthouse."

There were a few questioning expressions at hearing this statement, and the men looked at David with anticipation on their faces.

"Yes," David said, "the image of a lighthouse came to my mind even before I met Dr. Newcomb. It was as if the Lord was telling me that our church needed to be a shining light for the community. Would that work, Terry?"

"Yes! I do think a lighthouse will work," Terry replied, already running through a hundred possibilities in his mind. "I'll be happy to put together some designs in the next couple of weeks."

Pastor David walked back to the whiteboard with marker in hand and quickly sketched a lighthouse on the opposite side of the board from the field. In a happy, jumbled coincidence, the three signposts covered thus far created a path that ended with the lighthouse.

He looked at the picture and then stepped away from the board with a feeling of satisfaction. "Now what else can we do to really make this stick?" he said.

After brainstorming for a few minutes, Ralph raised his hand. Almost immediately, the group got silent as each man looked expectantly at him.

"Go ahead, Ralph," said David.

"Well . . . I think that marketing is fine for presentin' our ideas and all that, but we can't rely on fancy pictures when it comes to helpin' people really get involved, can we?"

He was about to sit down, but added, "No offense, Terry."

The young deacon grinned at this and assured the chairman that no offense was taken.

"Actually," Terry said, "You've made a good point, Ralph. I think that if the rest of the congregation is going to take hold of this plan, they're going to do it by following our example." Several of the men grunted their agreement at this, and Pastor David nodded his head approvingly.

"I have an idea!" announced one of the elders from the back of the table. "As long as we're goin' back to how Pastor Newcomb and his wife started things at the beginning, why don't we ask them to come and speak to the rest of the congregation along with us?"

"That makes sense," said Pastor David.

"We could present the whole idea on a Sunday

evening," chimed in another elder from the back, "and the Newcombs might be open to a visit."

"But we shouldn't advertise them," said another. "It would work best as a secret."

"Could we advertise some surprise guests?" asked yet another of the men, and on and on the conversation went.

David watched his fellow leaders contentedly for a few moments, and then walked to the whiteboard and filled in the fourth *R*.

SIGNPOST #4:
REORGANIZE OUR APPROACH TO THE COMMUNITY

After a few moments, the rest of the elders and deacons noticed that David was moving on, and they quieted down to let him explain the next principle.

"Based on what we learned from Ken Siever," David said, "and what we know about our own ministries, I don't think our community knows a whole lot about Midland Church." Several of the men sighed.

"So," David said with a smile, "we're going to have to figure out a way to introduce ourselves! Let's hear some ideas." Once again, the room buzzed with ideas and suggestions. After about 15 minutes, the group had produced a list of possibilities ranging from handing out tracts to bringing in a carnival to advertising in the yellow pages (Fred Turner growled audibly when the circus was suggested).

Watching it all happen, David felt a spring of hope welling up inside his heart. After all of the doubting and planning and hoping and praying, the leadership of Midland Church was excitedly brainstorming how to reach out to their community.

I can't wait to tell Ken all about it, David thought to himself, and then another idea popped into his mind.

"Please humor me, but by all means, follow me!" he announced loudly, abruptly charging through the doorway and into the hall. The elders and deacons jumped out of their chairs to follow. By the time the whole group had caught up to him, David was standing in the street at the intersection of 9th Ave. and Kearney—in the exact spot where Ken Siever had led him almost a month before.

"Can anyone tell me what our sign says?" asked David. He was immediately gratified to see the whole group of men squint into the sun and cup their hands above their eyes. One by one, each of the men agreed that the sign had to go.

"That's a pretty poor lighthouse sign," said Terry, and the others concurred.

"If you'll all follow me," David said, "we can look over some other things that need improve—" David stopped abruptly as Ralph leaned over and whispered into his ear. He then turned to the men and said, "You guys go ahead and explore the property on your own. Let's see what we can do to spruce up our lighthouse!"

With a laugh and a cheer, the men split up into groups and began canvassing the church grounds.

"Are you sure about this?" David asked Ralph when they were the only ones still standing in the street.

"Oh, yeah," replied Ralph with a chuckle. "Now that you've opened their eyes, you just watch them ol' boys go to work!"

He was right. As David and Ralph walked around the property, stopping for a few minutes with each group, David was amazed to see how enthusiastically the men—the deacons especially—dived into discovering the building's flaws.

Toolboxes and measuring tapes materialized out of thin air, along with pencils and notebooks to record each problem and detail the materials and time needed to fix it. It was as if these same leaders had just arrived from somewhere else to examine the church property for the first time. To David it seemed almost surreal.

"Remember," Pastor David called out to the men, "we can't do any major repairs until we present our ideas to the church. So for now we'll need to just get ready."

As Ralph and David finished their tour of the property, David remarked that he hadn't seen Fred in any of the groups.

"That's because he wasn't in any of the groups," Ralph replied, sighing heavily. "I saw him skip out when we all followed you into the street."

David looked toward the parking lot and saw that Fred's truck was missing.

"We're gonna have to deal with him sooner or later," Ralph said. "Ol' Fred is pretty much threatened by all this."

After about half an hour of watching the deacons swarm over the church grounds, David decided that it was useless to try to get everyone back into the conference room.

"I have to get ready for the evening service," he told Ralph. "Would you mind supervising things and making sure everyone is done before all the people start showing up?"

"Sure thing," replied the big man. "But what about your last *R*?"

"Well," David replied with a grin, "I guess we'll just have to have another meeting!"

CHAPTER 8

Counting the Cost

On the following Sunday afternoon, David arrived at the church about a half-hour before the next meeting began and was surprised to see the deacons measuring walls and windows. After looking around for a few moments, David spotted Ralph Nicholson, who had an earnest expression on his face.

"What's going on?" David asked Ralph after the two had shaken hands.

"Oh, the deacons just decided to get a few projects out of the way," said Ralph, looking a little embarrassed.

"Think we can keep it low profile?" David asked. A feeling of alarm prickled him. "We really should be cautious about doing any projects until after we explain everything to the rest of the congregation."

"I know, I know," said Ralph, slowly rubbing his hands together. "It's just that last week you opened these boys' eyes to how poor things'd gotten around here, and, well, they're just bitin' at the bit to get started, that's all."

David smiled ruefully. "But how much can they get done before the meeting starts?" he asked.

Once again, Ralph seemed embarrassed as he thought about his answer, and he began to rub his hands together a little faster.

"Well . . . actually, the deacons were thinkin' that maybe it would be better if they just got stuff done out here and let you, me and the elders figure out the rest inside."

"Ralph," David said gently, "I'm not sure that's the best strategy. If we get too far ahead of our church family, they may react adversely and even feel left out. And the truth is, we aren't quite ready to guide everyone through the rediscovery and rededication."

"Yep, I see your point," Ralph said. "We'll only get one chance to do it right."

"Trust me, Ralph," David said, patting him on the back. "After the big meeting we're going to have a lot of volunteers who want to help, so we need to leave some work for them." David gave his friend one last pat on the shoulder and walked into the church to work on yet another presentation to the leaders.

When David walked into the conference room, all of the deacons were seated around the table with the elders. He looked over at Ralph, who shot a glancing smile back and winked to show that the deacons were on the same page.

"All right," said David as he settled on his chair, "is everybody here?"

"Everyone but Fred," one of the elders chimed in. "He called me this afternoon and let me know that he was 'unavailable'."

"Okay," David said without further comment on Fred's absence. "I've prepared a little bit of a devotional that I'd like to share, if that's all right, Chairman Nicholson?"

Ralph chuckled at the Pastor's formality and nodded his head.

"Great! Then let's all turn in our Bibles to the book of Acts." After allowing a few moments for shuffling pages, David spent the next 20 minutes expounding on the world of the Early Church.

He started with the disciples in the upper room, scattered like sheep without a shepherd until the coming of the precious Holy Spirit. He read about Peter's sermon during Pentecost, and the 3,000 believers who were added to the Church that day. And he read about the healing of the lame beggar in the Temple, and the courage of Peter and John before the council of the Jewish leaders.

As he read, a palpable enthusiasm spread around the table. Each man felt the power involved in taking up the cause of the gospel, and each man caught a glimpse of the incredible boldness the Early Christians demonstrated as they spoke of Jesus in the midst of hostility. David felt it too as he read from the Scriptures, but he stopped abruptly and asked the men a question.

"How many of you can relate to the leaders of this Early Church?" he asked, "How many of you can feel their excitement?" About half of the leaders raised their hands. After a moment, the others followed suit until each hand was raised. David also raised his hand, but the smile on his face was grim, even troubling, as he met the eyes of his colleagues.

"Let's keep reading," he said, lowering his hand and his gaze to the pages of his Bible. He kept reading, although it soon became clear that the tenor of the Early Church changed.

David read about the deaths of Ananias and Sapphira, the couple who stained the purity of the Church with greed. Then there was the story of Stephen—a man who refused to abandon the gospel of Jesus Christ even as he was being stoned to death. And then Pastor David read of Saul and his persecution of the believers, along with the death of James and the imprisonment of Peter.

Slowly at first, but more quickly as David read on, the enthusiasm of the elders and deacons was replaced with tension. No longer did they casually enjoy their journey through the New Testament Church. No longer could they feel the power of the gospel. Now there was concern for the safety and integrity of the Early Church, and still David read on.

He read of the apostle Paul being stoned at Lystra, and then being beaten with rods and imprisoned, along with Silas, at Philippi. He read concerning the riot in Ephesus and of the angry mob of people swarming over the believers, shouting "Great is Artemis of the Ephesians!"

Around the table, the men held on to their Bibles, their eyes glued to the page as Pastor David read passage after passage.

He read of Paul being accosted by an angry mob in Jerusalem, and his subsequent arrest and confinement by the Roman Tribune. He read concerning the hatred of the Jewish leaders and their vow to never again taste food until Paul was dead. And he read of Paul's transfer to Rome, of the storm, the shipwreck, the snake bite, and on and on until the men around the table were almost certain that their pastor was undoubtedly preparing to make one colossal point!

The story of the Early Church continued with Paul's frustrations with the carnal Corinthians and the confused and manipulated Galatians.

Finally, with a heavy sigh, David concluded his tour of the Early Church and closed his Bible.

"How many of you can relate to the leaders of that Early Church?" he asked after a moment had passed. "How many of you can relate to the scorn and beatings and persecution?" No hands were raised. "Praise God that we live in a free country!"

Once again David allowed a moment to pass before continuing. "Midland Church is a New Testament church," he said in soft tone of voice. "We were founded by the same Holy Spirit as our predecessors, and our church started and grew with the same excitement. But then we got off track."

His gaze met the eyes of some of the older deacons and elders, all of whom nodded in recognition of their mistakes.

"We got off track, and we became less than a threat to the malignant forces of evil," David said, "and so we missed the persecution and the scorn and the suffering that's supposed to come when you follow Jesus."

This comment created a slight stir among the men in the room, and one elder observed, "Americans can hardly relate to persecution."

David then led them to Peter's writings. "Let me put

it this way: Motion causes friction. Anytime God's people make Kingdom gains, their efforts will not go unnoticed. There will be an inevitable reaction from Satan's realm."

As he spoke, he accentuated his words by pointing to a wooden cross hanging on the wall above the whiteboard.

"Last week was an important step for us as leaders of this church," he said, "because we decided and committed ourselves to lead our church back to the original track. Frankly, I couldn't be more excited, and I couldn't be more proud. BUT . . !" He startled several of the men close to him with the intensity of this exclamation. "If we do get ourselves—and our church—back on track, I feel that it's important for all of us to recognize *where that track leads*." David emphasized the last four words by thumping on his Bible four times with his open hand.

"So," David continued with a softer voice as he slid back into his chair, "before we talk about what our church can do to reconnect with the community, we need to make sure that all of our hearts are in the right place and that we're committed to finish what we've started even when things start getting tough."

As he finished speaking, David took a moment to collect his thoughts. He started to walk over to the whiteboard when a low, strong voice spoke up behind him.

"I'm committed, Pastor David," said Ralph

Nicholson. David turned around and smiled at his friend, truly touched. He had not actually expected any of the men to verbalize their commitment, but he felt it was a wonderful gesture on Ralph's part. He turned back toward the whiteboard, and once again he was interrupted.

"I'm committed, too." This came from Terry Sullivan, and the look on his face proved to everyone that he meant it.

"I'm committed," chimed in an elder on the left.

"Me too!" echoed another, and another, until each man at the table had voiced his accord with his pastor's words.

"Thank you, all," said David when they had finished. It was clear that he had been affected by their votes of commitment, and before he moved on he took in a deep breath to regain control of his emotions.

"Okay," he continued with only a slight crack in his voice, "let's figure out what exactly we're committed to!"

He erased the scribblings and doodles the children had left from their Sunday School class and looked back toward the group.

"As I said, we are a New Testament church, which means that we have the same job as Peter, Paul and Barnabus, and all of the leaders who got us to this point. So what were the attitudes and beliefs that helped them launch such an earth-changing revolution?"

Several of the men spoke up at once, and as they identified each trait, David listed it on the board in large block letters.

A DEEP LOVE FOR JESUS CHRIST
SUBMISSION TO HIS WILL
PASSION FOR THE GOSPEL MESSAGE
LOYALTY TO EACH OTHER
GENUINE CONCERN FOR THE LOST
RELIANCE ON THE HOLY SPIRIT
AN ABIDING FAITH IN JESUS
PRAYER WARRIORS!

In what seemed like no time at all, the whiteboard was full, and David stepped back to examine the list.

"All right," he said, nodding his head enthusiastically. "These are the things that are certainly true of our forefathers of the faith. They should also be true of us. Are we agreed?"

Each of the men around the table nodded his head in agreement. There was an energy building up again within the room, and they could all feel it.

Pastor David was a master at reaching down deep within a man. In reading so many Scriptures during their meeting, he had succeeded in leading each person on an emotional journey of discovery. Now they all had a clear picture of who they were and where they were going. They also had a much better understanding of the tremendous cost of true discipleship. There were no longer any illusions that spiritual leadership was a walk in the park. Better still, each leader had returned from Pastor David's grim journey of the book of Acts with the grit and fortitude to stay the course, regardless of the cost.

As the group sat and pondered this new feeling, David erased the whiteboard once again and wrote three questions.

"Okay," he said, taking a deep breath and steeling himself for the race to come. "In a few moments we need to start talking about some specific strategies for evangelism. But first I think we should pray."

The men quickly formed themselves into small groups of two or three. Ralph Nicholson joined with David, and as the two men got down on their knees, Ralph gave the young pastor an enthusiastic slap on the back.

"I always knew you were good," he said with a smile, "but that was somethin' else, brother." David smiled in return, and gave the big man a hardy slap of his own. "I'll thank God for that!" he said.

Then they bowed their heads and opened heaven with their prayers.

CHAPTER 9

Outreach Tools

After fervent prayer, David glanced at his watch and noticed that the evening service would begin in less than an hour.

"If everyone will take a seat," he called out to the elders and deacons, "we will get started again."

The men continued to mill around for a few moments, enjoying the fellowship, and then one by one returned to the table as David once again called out, "Back to the drawing board!"

After a brief swig from his water bottle, David strolled to the whiteboard. His eyes went to the cross hanging above the board.

You just have to stay centered on the cross, he reminded himself. *No matter how passionate toward any issue or opportunity the team becomes, stay connected to the cross, David!*

After another brief moment of reflection, he turned back toward the men, some of whom were still stretching their legs or grabbing a cup of coffee.

"Well, I certainly feel refreshed," he said to the whole group. From the bright smiles that spread across the faces of several of the men, he could see they felt the same.

"Now we need to get specific. How are we going to get the gospel out to our community?"

The deacons and elders suggested a flurry of ministry ideas, and David wheeled around to the board and furiously started writing down everything he heard.

Canvassing the neighborhoods with
a questionnaire
Memberships in the Lion's Club
Blue Grass musicals (Friday or Sunday
evenings)
Friend Day (Sunday morning annual
extravaganza)
Weekly home groups
Annual open house
Yellow Pages
Newspaper advertising
Passing out tracts at Wal-Mart

Cold turkey knocking on doors
Helping out at the local homeless mission
Marquee signage with changing messages
Bringing in well-known people to speak
Annual barbecue

After about 10 minutes, David's hand was in danger of cramping, so he asked the men to take a break from new ideas and discuss the suggestions already written on the board.

As ideas were tossed around and debated, Terry Sullivan began to feel that something was missing. He listened with interest as his friends and colleagues discussed the merits and disadvantages of each proposal; but as time went on, a picture began to form in his mind.

Children! he said to himself after a few moments of intense thinking. *Nobody is thinking about children and youth!*

At about the same time that Terry Sullivan had his epiphany, Pastor David came to a discouraging conclusion of his own. As he looked over the list of proposed evangelistic techniques and listened to the lively discussion several deacons were having about which day of the week would be best for a "Country Jesus Bluegrass Festival," it became clear that the leaders of Midland Church had little to no experience in evangelism. For many years, personal witnessing and church outreach had barely shown up on the church radar. When someone did muster the courage to share his or her faith, it was generally seen as a nice exception but never the rule or standard.

Of course, what was even more frustrating for the pastor was that he generally avoided witnessing to others himself. So here he stood, struggling over his own inadequacies while trying to lead others to a grand plan for the church. The observation hit him like a load of bricks. David realized that as pastor he had to be the standard bearer. It was as if the Lord was saying to him, "David, don't expect these men to do what you yourself are not willing to do."

Sighing, he picked up a colored marker and was about to call for more suggestions when Terry Sullivan raised his hand.

"Go ahead, Terry," Pastor David said, a little curious about the excited look on the young man's face.

"Well," Terry began, unconsciously borrowing Ralph Nicholson's favorite introduction, "I think we already have an extremely powerful tool right here in the church."

His comment elicited several surprised mutters and glances from the other men around the table, but Terry pressed on.

"We've had it for the past four years," he said, "but I don't think it has been used correctly."

"Well if we've had it for years," chirped one of the deacons who was a little miffed that his Bluegrass Festival had been so quickly cut off, "why hasn't it worked?" Several of the men grunted their agreement.

"Now hold on a minute," said Pastor David. "Let Terry finish his line of thought." He didn't know why, but he felt like the young deacon was on to something. Whether it was the Holy Spirit or just the earnestness in his face, a peculiar exhilaration began to well up inside of David that allowed him to hope the answer was about to come. "Go ahead, Terry," he said, trying not to appear too anxious.

"Awana," Terry said, simply.

"Awana?" said Pastor David, visibly confused and unable to hide it.

"Awana!" said Terry confidently.

David turned around to write the newest suggestion on the whiteboard, feeling very disappointed indeed. His hopes had vanished in a single word and now he wondered about Terry.

Maybe I can call Ken Siever, he thought to himself, and was actually about to suggest it to the group when one of the deacons spoke up.

"My sister's church has a huge Awana program," the deacon said, "and she says the congregation really grew once they started using Awana as an outreach tool."

"Yeah," echoed an elder sitting to the man's right. "We came from a church that ran Awana, and I actually had several friends who started attending because of their children. Imagine that! Children bringing their parents to church!"

"Wait a minute," said David. "Are you saying this children's ministry is actually a church evangelism tool?"

The leaders turned to each other as if struck by a strange revelation. Could a ministry for children and youth also be an actual evangelism instrument?

Other men began to recount their positive experiences with the Awana program, and fairly soon there was an unmistakable buzz around the table. Pastor David, however, remained unconvinced.

"But the earlier question still stands," he said, directing his question to Terry. "If we've had Awana for all these years, then why hasn't it worked already?"

"I think the main problem," Terry said, "is that we've been treating our Awana program like everything else in the church—it's all been inwardly focused."

Several members of the group agreed with this assessment and began discussing how such an error could have occurred.

"What about our visitation program?" said another man. It was Bill Campbell, a deacon who had a gift of gab and loved to use it witnessing to people. "Visitation began as opportunities to share Christ with the guests who had come to our church services. Now we only go see people who are members but haven't been to church in years. We aren't reaching out to anyone; we're only trying to get back those who have no interest in coming here, while the ones who have visited are forgotten."

The chain reaction among the men was startling. Terry's observation about how Awana had been corrupted to focus inward to the point of being nearly unrecognizable to its original intent led others to sort through the files of their memories to discover other corruptions. When Bill finished with his diagnosis of the visitation program, another man mentioned the music and how his grandkids weren't coming any more because, while they loved the hymns, they also enjoyed newer songs of faith. Still another deacon observed that the ushers never greeted the few new faces that came through the door but seemed to have endless time to "flap" with their friends in the church. The bulletin, the activities—it seemed the list of what no longer resembled its original intent was endless.

It began to dawn on these men that when they had begun to allow the church to focus inwardly, they had allowed a cancer to invade their ministry that had corrupted every program and service within the Body. It appeared that nothing that began as an outreach to guests or the community now functioned as such.

"We don't need new ministries," Terry said. "We need to reclaim the old ones." This truth settled on them all, and there was a palpable sense of guilt for having let things slip so far from their original purpose.

"We need to roll up our sleeves and get done what needs gettin' done," Ralph Nicholson said. "There's really nothin' to lose. We're already runnin' these programs and doin' these ministries, so all that's needed is for us to start doin' 'em right and see what happens!"

Hearing this, David leaned against the wall and thoughtfully tapped his finger to his chin. "That's a good point, Ralph," he mused. "I guess that settles it!"

Just as David was beginning to get excited over the possibilities in the ministries he had so wanted to be rid of shortly before, an elder sitting next to Terry spoke up.

"Well, if we're going to set these ministries straight, the first thing we have to do is find the right Awana Commander. Sheryl Smith is our current Awana Commander, and she and her husband are moving out of state at the end of the month!"

Several of the men frowned at this, glancing at each other thoughtfully for several moments.

Ralph Nicholson had a different reaction, however. A broad grin spread across his face, and he stood up and clasped his hands behind his back.

"I would like to make a proposal," he said in a deep, commanding voice. "I propose that this Board appoint Terry Sullivan as the next Awana Commander of Midland Church!"

David had become very close friends with Ralph over the course of the past few months, and he was aware that the big man knew how to strike when the iron was hot.

"I second the nomination," replied the elder who had delivered the news of the Smith family's impending exodus.

"Any discussion?" Ralph said.

No one spoke for the single second it took for Ralph to move things forward at lightning speed.

"Shall we take a vote?" he boomed, speaking in his most formal and authoritative voice. "All in favor . . . ?"

"Aye!" came the resounding reply of the group.

"All opposed . . . ?" said Ralph. As he looked around for several seconds before proclaiming that the motion had carried, several men reached over to shake Terry's hand.

"Congratulations, Terry," said Pastor David. "But I guess we should ask you if you want the job?"

"Well . . . I'm flattered," said Terry after taking a moment to catch his breath, "but are you sure I'm the right man?"

"We're sure!" said Ralph, whose voice was followed by a chorus of amens.

"Terry," chimed in Pastor David, "I think it's pretty

clear that God has raised you up for such a time as this. If you're right about the potential of this ministry, then I think this is a pretty exciting time for our church, and for you personally."

"Yeah," said Terry, after taking a deep breath. "Yeah! I'll do it!"

His acceptance was greeted with a warm round of applause from the group. As David clapped, he looked over at the clock on the wall and gasped.

"Whoa!" he said, "We've only got five minutes left before the evening service starts. We've gotta wrap this up!"

Ralph Nicholson called for the meeting to adjourn, which was quickly seconded and the vote passed. As the men filed out of the conference room, several of them patted Terry on the back or ruffled his hair in a congratulatory gesture. David personally loved this Southern custom of patting each other's backs—a genuine form of affirmation and kinship.

When the last of the deacons had left the room, David went up to Terry and said, "Are you nervous at all?"

"I guess a little bit," Terry replied, bashfully rubbing his cheek.

"That's okay," said David encouragingly. "The most important thing to remember is that you're not on your own. I'm here to help any time you need me.

Seriously, I'm here to serve you; and as we seek the Lord together, I'm sure that He will keep both of us on the right path."

"Thanks, Pastor David," Terry replied, shaking his pastor's hand and feeling a strong sense of affirmation. He started to walk out the door but then stopped abruptly.

"Actually," he said, "that reminds me; I think I read somewhere that the senior pastor of a church is also the head of the Awana program."

David raised his eyebrows in mild surprise. "Really?" he asked. But Terry only shrugged his shoulders.

"I'm not exactly sure," Terry said as he walked out the door, "but I'll find out and let you know."

David heard a barely suppressed chuckle behind him and turned to see Ralph Nicholson bowled over at the waist in laughter.

"Not sure what you got yourself into, are ya?" asked the big man, still trying not to laugh, but failing miserably.

"We'll see," said Pastor David, unable to keep from smiling. "We will just have to see. However, I do want to work with you and the leaders to come up with three additional outreach vehicles, besides this kids' program, that will help us engage Midland again." With that, the two men walked out the door and into the sanctuary.

In the room just vacated was a lonely *R* written on the bottom of the whiteboard, unnoticed by the men throughout the meeting and—for now—unexplored.

CHAPTER 10

Captain David

David Newman often referred to his wedding day as the best day of his life. There would never come a sunset when he hadn't thanked the Lord for blessing him with such a wonderful woman as Catherine. Truly, more than any other earthly thing, she was his heart and soul. From the moment they met she had been his best friend and wisest counsel. And in that capacity, she very often surprised him.

"What's wrong, David?" Catherine asked her husband, two days after the latest meeting of the church leaders.

"Why do you think anything's wrong?" David responded, sounding a bit sullen and childish without realizing it.

"Because you're picking at your food like a four-year-old who doesn't like vegetables."

David looked down at his plate for a moment and then raised his head with a bashful smile.

"Ish dat beddah?" he asked after taking a large mouthful of roast beef and mashed potatoes.

"Don't be gross!" Catherine admonished, trying not to snicker.

David shoveled a spoonful of peas in his mouth and said, "Ah surely wuv you!" He batted his eyes and folded his hands together in front of his face.

Catherine burst into a gale of laughter that warmed her husband's heart more than a mountain of mashed potatoes ever could.

"Seriously," she said, wiping her eyes, "what's wrong?"

David sighed and pushed back from the table to stand up.

"I'm not sure. I think I've made a decision that's going to be unpopular with the deacons and elders, but it's best for the church."

"What decision?" Catherine said in mild surprise. David had always included her in his ministry plans, and it was unusual for him to make big decisions without talking to her first.

"Well . . . I think I'm going to cut the Awana program." After saying this, he brought his hands to his chest in a defensive posture. Catherine remained silent, however, which David interpreted as an encouraging sign.

"I just think it's going to be a waste of time," he said, starting to pace. "My plan would be to take the dozen or so Awana leaders and train them in evangelism. That way we're not dependent on bringing in more children from the community, and we can go straight to the adults." Once more he stopped to let his wife interject her opinion, and once more she remained silent. This time, David began to think that her silence was not so encouraging after all.

"It's not that kids aren't important," he said into the awkward silence. "It's just that adults are more . . . well, *more* important, aren't they?"

Catherine seemed to be lost in thought, and after only a few moments, David could stand it no longer. "Won't you please tell me what you think?" he said.

Catherine gently dabbed the corners of her mouth with her napkin and then folded it on her lap. Still silent, she formed a tripod by resting her elbows on the table and propping her chin on top of her interlaced fingers.

"That probably ranks as the most unintelligent idea you've ever voiced," Catherine said flatly.

David's mouth elongated into an "O" of surprise.

"What do you mean?" he demanded, feeling a bit shaken, as he walked back to his chair.

"I mean that it's just a horrible idea!" she said.

"First of all, adults are *not* more important than children! Just because grown-ups contribute to the offering doesn't mean they're more worthy of salvation—or more easily saved! In fact, they're far more resistant to the gospel. And second of all—" She stopped and took a deep breath to quench the fire rising in her throat.

"Second of all," she said, more calmly, "we're trying to build a church that will grow for many years, not do some kind of evangelistic sprint. We need to stop dismissing children's ministry and start making it our top priority!"

"But we have Sunday School," David said. "Isn't that enough for children?"

"I think you're missing the boat, David. Proverbs 22:6 is a mandate to parents. When will the church start pushing back when dads and moms leave their children on the church doorstep with every expectation that the church is responsible for their kid's spiritual formation?"

"Hold on now!" interjected David. "Discipleship for adults and children is a whole different subject. Let's stick with evangelism. And that's my point; I just can't see how a children's club is going to help us evangelize Midland! All of the deacons and elders seem to have a cousin's-brother's-wife's-sister who has seen Awana work, but none of them know how to get *our* program to work any more than I do!!!" As he spoke, he picked up his fork and petulantly pushed around a piece of broccoli on his plate.

"Well," Catherine said, still resting her head on her hands. "What did the materials say?"

"Which materials?"

"The Awana materials that Sheryl Smith brought over here last night."

David cleared his throat.

"I haven't read them—yet," he said at length.

"David!" Catherine caught herself in mid-scold. After shaking her head ever so slightly, she took another cleansing breath and walked over to where her husband sat and tenderly put her hands on his shoulders.

"Sweetheart," she began, causing him to look up at her with expectant eyes. "I think I know what's going on here." As she spoke, she slid into the chair next to him and took hold of his hand and looked into his eyes.

"How did things go at the meeting last week?" she asked.

"It was wonderful!"

"And are you still planning on making your presentation to the congregation?"

He answered by nodding his head slowly.

"Do you think," she continued, after bringing his hand to her lips and kissing it softly, "do you think that maybe you're feeling a little restless right now because you have all these exciting things you want to do with the church, but you have to wait until the church meeting before you can even think about doing them?"

Her husband sighed and pulled her hand to his own lips.

"That's a possibility," he conceded.

"And is it possible," Catherine continued, "that you might be a little nervous about how the meeting is going to go?"

Once again David nodded his head, and once again he kissed her hand.

"Okay," she said, even more gently. "I think that means the best thing for you to do right now is get your mind off of it. And I think the best way to do that is to buckle down and read those Awana materials and figure out how that ministry is supposed to work. It just may be that Awana has purposefully been held back by some well-meaning people."

Without waiting for an answer, she squeezed his hand and then walked to the sink to begin washing the dishes.

David remained in his chair for a minute, thinking about what his wife had said. Finally he got up from the table and went to stand beside her.

"Thank you, honey," he said. "You really are a discerning woman."

Catherine hugged him fiercely in response, and

then David went to his study to grapple with the Awana guidebooks.

After about an hour, Catherine checked on him and found him leaning back comfortably in his chair and leafing through a spiral book titled *Basic Training Manual*.

"Terry was right," David said, looking up. "This is nothing like the Awana we've been running at Midland Church."

"Is that a good thing?" Catherine asked.

"It's very good to know that we can use this," he said, giving the manual a little shake, "but it's disappointing to see how far off the mark we've been." He sighed heavily and put the manual facedown on the desk. "I just don't understand what happened. If anything, Awana is designed to be the superevangelistic tool of an outward focused church."

Catherine was about to make a suggestion when David held up his hand to stop her.

"I've got a grand thought," he said, thinking back to his first visit with the Awana program all those months ago. "Let's go drop in on Terry and Heather. I need to show Terry what I've found."

When there was no answer at the Sullivans' house, David and Catherine counted the days and realized that Terry and Heather were most likely at Awana. It was 7:30 P.M., and another hour remained before the end of the club night. They jumped into their car and made a dash for the church.

David found Terry observing the *Truth and Training* handbook time.

"Why, hello, Pastor!" Terry said. "What brings you out tonight?"

"I was reading the *Basic Training* manual, and I think you're right on," David said. The men walked out of the room and strolled with no particular direction in mind. From the edge of the auditorium and down the hallway into the makeshift gym erected in the fellowship hall, they caught a heated discussion going on.

"Isn't that Fred Turner's voice?" Terry said.

Pastor David nodded, feeling a cold knot form in the pit of his stomach. "Let's go find out for sure," he said.

When the two men entered the gym, they saw that it was Fred all right, flailing his arms to punctuate his words. He had corralled Sheryl Smith under one of the basketball hoops, and was shouting at her. Neither David nor Terry could hear what was being said at first, but as they drew near, it became obvious that Fred was not pleased.

"Hi, Fred," said David loudly when he and Terry had come within 20 feet of the deacon. Fred spun around and let out a surprised "Whoa!" Then his lip curled in an unconscious snarl.

"Hiya, Pastor Dave . . . Terry," said Fred, visibly trying to get control of himself.

"What's going on?" David asked.

"Oh, not much," Fred replied, glancing back and forth between Sheryl and Terry. "I was just explaining to Mrs. Smith about the Board's decision to have Mr. Sullivan here come in as the next Commander."

One look at Sheryl's face convinced Pastor David that Fred had been doing a little more than "explaining."

"And I was just *explaining* to Mr. Turner," retorted Sheryl, "that you already called me and filled me in about Terry and that I think it's a great idea!" She spoke these last words looking directly at Fred, who retreated a few steps toward the door.

"Actually, I think it's great that you're both here," said Terry, "because Pastor David and I are trying to do a bit of research to understand the Awana program a little better."

Pastor David reached into his backpack and pulled out the *Basic Training Manual.* As soon as Sheryl saw it, her face brightened.

"There's some good stuff in there, huh!" Sheryl said, looking at Pastor David.

"Yes there is," he responded, "but it's a little different from what we do here, don't you think?"

Sheryl nodded her head vigorously and was about to respond when Fred jumped in.

"Well, you know these manuals," he said, folding his hands together and lowering his head in a fawning way. "They kinda give the main points, but it's really up to the church to use it the way they want to."

Terry spoke up. "What we're curious about is the lack of evangelism here. It seems pretty clear from the manuals that Awana is supposed to be used as a tool to reach the community around the church and bring in new members, but I've looked through the attendance records over the past few years and we just haven't been doing that." His comment was directed toward Fred, but it was Sheryl who broke in with the answer.

"You're right about Awana," she said. "It's supposed to help bring new children into the church, and that's what we used to do here a long time ago. I know, because my daughter came about 15 years ago, and that's how we got involved with this church."

Fred eyed her coldly, but she pressed on.

"It's only been in the past five years or so that things have changed," she said.

"And why did they change?" Pastor David asked intently.

"Well," she replied, glancing toward Fred, "some of the church leadership thought it would be a better idea if we focused Awana just on the children of church members."

David sighed and pulled on his right ear thoughtfully as he looked over at Fred, who was turning an astonishing shade of red. In that moment the errant pieces to a disturbing puzzle came together. David now understood what—and who—had been responsible for cutting the legs out from under the Awana program and focusing it inward. He stole a quick glance at Terry, who gave a slight nod to show that he understood.

"Well, that's all changed now," David said, returning his attention to Sheryl. "We're going to get Awana back on its feet. And, of course the church leadership is united in that goal. Right, Fred?"

If it was possible for the deacon to turn any redder, he did so, then muttered his disgust with the conversation and bolted for the door. Sheryl was visibly shaken as she watched him go. She turned back to Pastor David and tried to speak, but the words would not come. As tears welled up in her eyes, she gave each gallant rescuer a hug while croaking out a heartfelt thank-you.

"Try not to worry about him," Pastor David said, doing his best to put her at ease. "We have more important things to talk about right now, like getting this program back to where it's supposed to be."

As David led Terry and Sheryl up the stairs and into the church office, he said, "Do you really think this can work, Sheryl?"

"Oh yes!" she replied enthusiastically. "The Awana program is what got my children coming here at first—and then they brought me and my husband!"

David was about to ask another question when Sheryl continued speaking.

"I also think Awana is a great discipleship tool," she said. "We not only worked hard to disciple our children but we also used to have the high school youth group volunteer as Awana leaders, and they built some good relationships with the younger kids and became good role models for them." As she spoke, Sheryl looked up at the ceiling, as if reading some kind of inverted teleprompter.

"Anything else?" asked Terry encouragingly.

"Oh yes!" Sheryl responded again. "A lot of times the high schoolers would become good friends with some of the adult leaders, and we even had a few mentoring relationships develop."

Sheryl's tone became apologetic as she said, "Pastor, my hands have been tied. Fred is not the only one dead set against this church growing. I can't begin to tell you how grateful I am to God for you!" As she finished speaking, she looked expectantly at Terry and Pastor David.

"The more I hear, the more I like," said David, thoughtfully. "Terry, didn't you tell me that the pastor is supposed to serve as the head of Awana?"

"It's in the book!" Terry replied. "Your first job is to

be the captain of the Awana troops, so to speak." He chuckled at his own analogy until he saw the confused glance on the pastor's face.

"Basically," Terry said, "your job is to make sure that Awana stays on course and keeps functioning correctly. And then you are encouraged to develop relationships with the leaders and parents."

Terry's face grew even more animated as he said, "But most of all, Pastor David, you have an army of dedicated volunteers who are willing to be led into spiritual battle. Will you do that for us?"

David felt a stab of shame. Only a short while ago, he had announced to Catherine his plan to dump the ministry of Awana because he wanted a team of dedicated Christians who would reach out and engage the community with him. To his utter amazement, his army was already in motion. They were here tonight—serving, and waiting for their captain!

Suddenly Sheryl looked down at her watch and squeaked in dismay.

"Oh! The kids'll be back in the gym any moment!"

"Thank you, Sheryl!" Terry and Pastor David called after her as she scuttled through the door.

"Still up to the challenge?" David asked, extending a hand across his desk to his new leader of Awana.

Terry grinned and vigorously shook the pastor's hand.

"Let's go get 'er done!" he exclaimed.

David grinned at the young deacon. "And I promise that my wife and I will be right here every week."

"Sounds good, Captain!" Terry replied. "By the way, I'll bet there are some parents picking up their kids as we speak. Should we go introduce ourselves?"

David laughed again and then inclined his head.

"After you, Commander!" he said and followed his good friend down the stairs and into the gym—and out into uncharted waters.

CHAPTER 11

Congregational Meeting

As Dolores Jenkins approached the sanctuary the following Sunday evening, she was feeling more excited than she had ever felt about attending a church service, and her heart fluttered within her chest as she looked around for her friends. Spotting Betty Salina off to the left, she quickly deposited her husband at the end of a nearby pew and hurried over to scout for any news.

"Tom and I just got back from Florida," she announced breathlessly after giving her friend a quick hug. "What did we miss this morning?"

"Not much," announced Betty in a mysterious whisper. "Pastor David just said that he and the church leaders were ready to make their big announcement tonight, and that he hoped everybody would come!"

"Ooooh, my!" Dolores squealed in excitement, and then her voice quickly descended in volume to her own version of a mysterious whisper. "Tom said that Bill Hatcher told him something about special visitors tonight—is that true?'

"Oh, yes!" Betty replied, and then lightly bonked herself on the head as a reprimand for her own forgetfulness. "Pastor David said there will be two surprise guests tonight, but he wouldn't say who they were."

Dolores was almost overcome by this nugget of information and was forced to hold on to the pew in front of her as she processed it.

By this time, several other women had heard Dolores's animated squeal and had hurried over to see if she had acquired some new piece of information.

"What do you suppose the announcement is going to be?" asked one of them in a hushed manner.

"Well," replied Dolores, authoritatively placing her hand on her hip, "I think the Board's approved a building project!"

Gasping in response to this revelation, several of the women joined Dolores in reaching for the back of the pew and shuffled closer to her, much like birds clustering together on a telephone wire.

"They wouldn't do that!" exclaimed one of the ladies. "Our elders and deacons most certainly would get a consensus from the church first."

"Well, have you seen all the new people around here?" peeped another. "Maybe it has something to do with a new gym!"

"No, no, no," chided Betty, shaking her head, "They're not building a gym." She busied herself in her purse after saying this, and the little crowd was silent for several moments until one of the women at the end could stand it no longer.

"Well, then, what on earth are they doing?!" Several others began to prod Betty when she still didn't answer.

"If you must know," Betty said, after fishing out some nondescript item, "my husband heard—*from one of the Board members himself*—that the church is going to sponsor some kind of lighthouse!"

"A lighthouse?! What would we ever do with a lighthouse?" This sent all of the women into a flurry as they rustled their purses.

When Pastor David stepped to the podium, Delores called, "They're starting!" and each woman fluttered back to find her husband and report the new intelligence before the meeting officially began.

Watching all of this with an optimistic smile, Pastor David looked over to Catherine for one more connection before launching the evening. The congregation settled into their seats looking up at him expectantly.

"I want to thank you all for coming," he said,

grasping the podium on both sides. "Let's begin with a time of prayer." Bowing his head, Pastor David thanked the Lord for Midland Church and asked for wisdom to be granted to everyone in the room as they discussed the future. His words were calm and softly spoken.

Before the prayer was finished, five individuals made their way into the auditorium. The only seating still available was on the front row near the piano. Two of the group carried a large bundle. Fred Turner, who was the last to find a seat, frowned at the praying pastor as he sat down.

"In Jesus' name we pray, amen," said David.

When the congregation opened their eyes, they could see that Ralph Nicholson had joined their pastor at the podium.

"Well, folks," began Ralph, as Pastor David sat down, "I know you're all anxious to hear what we've got to say, but we want to make sure that our heavenly Father is at the center of this whole thing, so let's worship Him before we do anything else."

The piano player began the prelude to "Holy, Holy Holy" even before Ralph finished speaking, and the congregation stood to sing.

David closed his eyes for a moment and allowed the words of the familiar hymn wash over him like a spring rain. An overwhelming sense of joy flooded his soul as he looked out over the church family. Then Fred caught the corner of his eye. David distinctly remembered not seeing Fred and his cluster of followers when he began his opening prayer. But here they were, bigger than life! No doubt, Fred had an agenda tonight. He had been conspicuously absent from the church for weeks. Now, instead of singing, Fred kept his eyes fastened defiantly on David.

Oh, Lord, David pleaded, *not tonight.* His breath caught in his chest for a moment as fear gripped him. In desperation David did the only thing he could do. He lifted up his anguish, along with all hope for the church family, and placed it squarely in the hands of Jesus. Slowly, he felt courage and conviction flow into his mind and body, filling every part of him and pushing away all fear and doubt.

"Thank you, Jesus," he whispered. A joyful smile spread across his face as he sang with all his might to the Lord. When the singing was finished, David returned to the podium and once again addressed the congregation.

"Ladies and gentlemen," he said with confidence, "I love our church, and I love all of you. And I think this is going to be one of the most memorable nights in our history." Several members of the congregation (including Dolores Jenkins) murmured excitedly upon hearing this, and Pastor David held up his hand before going on.

"This evening is the result of a number of fascinating events. Let me begin with the important visitor who came to our church well over a month ago. And I might add that he was a very interesting man indeed . . ."

For the next 15 minutes, Pastor David told his story. It began with Ken Siever and ended with the last meeting of the elders and deacons. The young pastor told the story with such a humble earnestness that (almost) no heart was left untouched when he had finished.

For David, this had been the hardest part of the evening to prepare for. He knew that he needed to make the congregation fully aware that years ago they had lost their way and it was time to reclaim their heritage. This had to be done even at the risk of offending some people. However, he also knew that camping out for very long on the shortcomings of the church would only produce a negative reaction, and then no change would take place at all. In the end, Catherine had served as his "emotional consultant," and as David looked out at the pliant faces, he could see that her service had been invaluable.

"I know that change can be difficult," continued David, "but this church has been blessed with some excellent leaders, and we have an exciting plan to share with you this evening." When he signaled to the soundboard, the sound technician pushed a few buttons and a colorful PowerPoint display popped up on the sanctuary wall behind the young pastor. The first slide showed a picture of Midland Church in autumn.

The crowd went wild! Power Point and large screens had never been used in their small church before, and the entire congregation buzzed with excitement for several minutes. David delighted in their enthusiasm. Ralph winked and held both thumbs up in the air toward David. This had been planned just between the two of them, and even the rest of the elders and deacons were pleasantly surprised.

"Our plan consists of five signposts to guide us," David continued once the congregation had settled down, "and I like to think of them as illuminated lampposts on the heavenly road." As he spoke, he once again signaled the technician, and the picture of the church dissolved into a large sketch of a street sign. At the top of the sign, three words were written in large block letters.

REDISCOVER OUR PURPOSE

"Our first signpost helps us to rediscover why this church came into being in the first place. The best part about this step is that it's already been done! The purpose of this church was recorded almost 40 years ago by its founding pastor, Dr. Daniel Newcomb."

This honored name was greeted by several hearty amens. David nodded toward the back of the church, where the head usher was waiting with a few other men and a large stack of papers.

Taking his cue, the head usher prompted four other men, and all of them began handing out documents down each of the aisles.

"Right now," said Pastor David, "our ushers are distributing the original constitution of Midland Church, written by Dr. Newcomb himself, so that you can all read and understand why we are here!" It took several moments for the ushers to get copies of the constitution to everybody. David waited patiently at the podium until everyone had a chance to begin reading.

Unfortunately, the ensuing pause was exactly what Fred Turner had been waiting for, and he did not waste his chance.

"Ladies and gentlemen!" he boomed, standing up and raising his hands. "Some of us have a problem with this here meetin' tonight. I encourage all y'all not to listen to this man! He does not have your best interest in mind!"

Immediately the entire room fell silent. People who had been reading the constitution and chattering enthusiastically now broke off talking and stared at the deacon, who still stood with his arms raised as if he were a modern-day prophet.

Dumbfounded, David could do little more than stare at Fred from the pulpit.

"You all know me," Fred said in his loudest and most authoritative voice. "You all know the things I've done for this church, and y'all know how long I've been around here doin' 'em." He spoke directly to the congregation and did not even glance in Pastor David's direction.

"This new Pastor's got himself a lot of fancy words talkin' about changin' everything, but I don't believe fancy words have gotten us where we are today—and I say, if it ain't broke . . ."

"DON'T FIX IT!" shouted the four individuals who had come into the church with Fred.

As if on cue, Fred reached under the pew and pulled out a large sign taped to garden stakes.

"If it ain't broke . . ." he roared once again, and then his posse roared back "DON'T FIX IT!" and pumped their sign wildly in the air.

Thinking back over the incident several years later, David realized that it was the sign that bothered him the most. It seemed impossibly large and was poorly painted with conflicting colors and outrageous slogans like "Midland Church Is Not Broken," and "Just Say No To Newman!"

The unexpected storm of Fred and his followers left David unable to speak—and let Fred continue unopposed for several moments.

"What this man wants," Fred sneered, pointing a finger in David's direction but still not deigning to look at him, "is to drag in any ol' Joe Schmoe from off the street and sit him down in your seat on Sunday mornin' in the middle of your family—in the middle of YOUR family!"

Several members of the congregation looked suspiciously around them upon hearing this, as if they were trying to catch a glimpse of this sinister individual before he could invade their space.

"This man thinks," Fred continued, still with a bent finger pointed in David's direction, "that if we don't get more folks in here, then we can't worship right! But I say that we've worshiped just fine for years without him around. And I say, if it ain't broke . . ."

"DON'T FIX IT!!!"

Fred and the four repeated this mantra three more times.

Both David and Ralph Nicholson watched in silent horror. It wasn't that they were incapacitated with paralyzing fear. It was the spectacle itself. Fred and his band of antagonists were so energized by their anger as to be almost comical.

Ralph desperately wanted to yell at Fred or maybe grab him by the scruff of the neck in front of the whole congregation. In a weak moment, Ralph felt that someone should apply the "right *fist* of fellowship" directly to Fred's nose. But he kept his hands glued to his side while his tongue felt as if were stuck to the back of his throat. He managed to keep his cool.

The outpouring of hostilities was briefly interrupted by the normally mild head usher, who swelled with righteous indignation. He had almost finished his job handing out copies of the constitution when Fred had launched his verbal assault. He found himself trapped and paralyzed, of all places, right in front of the older deacon. Fred's timing had unfortunately caught him standing at the front of the church, the very place he surely did not want to be. Quivering in fear, he thought it best to run as he was shouted at again and again with the words of Fred's mantra.

Finally, in a paroxysm of sheer panic, the usher rushed forward and handed Fred a copy of the old church constitution. Then, mercifully discharged of his duty, he ran for the rear of the sanctuary and collapsed lengthwise onto one of the pews like an exhausted marathon runner.

The congregation cheered and Fred was temporarily silenced as he looked down at the packet of papers in his hand and for a moment paused as if he had been hit by some kind of holy dart. It took a couple of glances to recognize the document. Then he raised the papers high in the air.

"And I don't need a paper required by the government to tell me how this church is s'posed to run!" he cried. "What's wrong with stickin' to the Scriptures?"

Then Fred tore the Constitution in half—and the silence of the crowd tore with it. Instantly the sanctuary erupted into groans and shouts as each member of the congregation stood up in defiance.

Still glued to the podium, Pastor David leaned into the microphone, and with enough volume to overtake Fred, he firmly said. "Please, *everyone,* sit down!"

David's words had little effect. Fred was still yelling and most people were talking back, crying out at the calamity or simply standing there enjoying the entertainment. This would certainly go down in history as one of the most exciting services in the history of Midland Church.

Fred had come that evening to stop Pastor David in his tracks. He had convinced himself that his stand against David and the church leaders was righteous, and that God expected him to make a stand. After all, he was fighting for his version of the life of the church. And so here he stood, unwilling to yield ground to this pastor—that wolf in sheep's clothing.

"The pastor asked everyone to sit down!" came a voice from the back of the auditorium. It was a loud but eloquent voice, and most everyone turned to see if the owner could be identified.

CHAPTER 12

Return to the Vision

I SAID, SIT DOWN!" boomed the mysterious visitor from the shadows once again. To David, at least, it seemed like the voice of God. It had come from behind the congregation, and as he squinted his eyes against the overhead lights, David could identify a figure standing beside the last pew.

The people in the congregation immediately found their places and plopped down. It was a loud but eloquent voice, and most everyone turned to see if the owner could be identified. In fact, a few unfortunate individuals had been standing in the aisles at this command and quickly found themselves desperately searching for any available seat.

Like everyone else, Fred had been stunned into

silence when the powerful voice rang out. But now, as he watched his control over the congregation slip away, his anger returned and brought more words with it.

"Just who do you think you are?" he demanded, taking a few steps toward the person and pushing his sleeves up as if preparing for a fight.

"Mind your tone, Fred Turner," replied the stranger, his voice still full of thunder. "You have dishonored me and you have dishonored God's people tonight!"

He took a step forward out of the shadow and was instantly illuminated by the lights of the sanctuary. A gasp went through the congregation as they recognized the man. Several of the older members began to clap—timidly at first, but then louder and bolder as more and more people joined in the applause. Soon everyone stood and began clapping wildly, and several of the men and women wiped tears from their cheeks.

"Ladies and gentlemen," said the pastor, "I would like to present our special guests for this evening—Dr. and Mrs. Daniel Newcomb!" Mary appeared after this introduction and took her place at her husband's elbow. The congregation increased the fervor of its applause with an immense crescendo as the old couple slowly made their way to the front.

Dr. Newcomb finally had to hold up his hand when it appeared the applause might not stop. From the moment his first words he had rung out, he had not taken his eyes off of Fred Turner. Now he addressed the deacon once again.

"How dare you make a mockery of this night!" he said sternly but quietly in an effort to save Fred any further embarrassment. "How dare you make a mockery of this place!"

Fred drew himself up like a turkey fluffing its feathers at the sound of a call. "You don't know nothin' of this place!" he replied, spitting out the words. "Not anymore. You may have got things started, but I've been runnin', I mean, I've been seein' to things for the past 15 years."

"And look what you've done!" cried Dr. Newcomb, pointing to the shredded Church Constitution still clutched in Fred's hands. "You've torn the heart out of this church and left it sick and dying."

Fred looked down at the tattered document in his hands and then dropped it with a grimace of horror as if he feared it might burst into flames.

"The whole thing's useless now," Fred said, looking down at the scattered papers at his feet. "What you wrote was fine to start things out, but it don't apply any more! Not with us!"

"Fred," replied Dr. Newcomb on a sigh, "when you first came to Midland Church, you were wounded and hurting. We took you in and loved you back to the Lord. But Fred, you never gave up your bitterness."

The deacon bristled at this, but Dr. Newcomb didn't allow him a chance to respond.

"Hebrews 12:15 tells us that God gives grace to his children, but if they turn from his grace a root of bitterness springs up to cause trouble."

"I ain't bitter!" Fred exclaimed. "I'm tryin' to save these people from makin' a bad mistake."

"Yes, Fred, you are bitter," Dr. Newcomb replied. "And not only that, but your bitterness has forced you to control this church."

Fred pointed to David. "No! He's tryin' to control everything!"

"God is taking control again," said Dr. Newcomb, "and you need to listen."

Amens and words of affirmation flooded the room.

"This church, or any other church," he continued, "exists to spread the Good News of Jesus Christ. That is our Great Commission, and that is our most solemn duty. We are God's lighthouse in Midland!" He began to move closer to Fred as he said this, causing Fred to retreat several steps.

"That's not my job!" Fred said with agitation in his voice.

"What you have done," said Dr. Newcomb, his eyes still locked on his target, "is abandon your first love for a little bit of security. That never works, because Jesus alone is our security. That's where faith comes in.

You replaced the wonderful purpose and vision of this church for a self-imposed fortress to protect yourself from being hurt again. And I WILL NOT STAND FOR IT ANY LONGER!"

Dr. Newcomb had continued to advance as he spoke, and this final burst was delivered within five feet of Fred.

The words struck the angry deacon as if they were an open palm, and he retreated an additional few paces before planting his feet and ruffling himself up again in opposition to the older man. Incredibly, he turned to Pastor David for support.

"Do you hear the way he's talkin' to me?" whined Fred, looking plaintively at the minister. "Are you just gonna stand there and listen to him berate one of the leaders of this church?"

David was temporarily struck dumb again by this tactic. He resisted the urge to laugh or to lower himself to Fred's level of destructive behavior. Instead, David cleared his throat to answer, and all eyes in the sanctuary (including Dr. Newcomb's) were on him.

"Fred, there's still room here tonight for you to make this right," he said. "You've made a mistake and sinned by not following the Matthew 18 principle; but you can still turn back. It's not too late."

Fred's pleading face twisted in disgust when David refused to get caught up in his ploy.

"Listen to him, Fred," said Dr. Newcomb softly.

The deacon wheeled about at the sound of the older man's voice.

"The path you've started down is a destructive one— I know, because I've seen where it leads—and you won't get many more opportunities to find your way back."

"Well that's mighty poetic of ya, Doc," Fred sneered in response to the older man's words and then turned his attention back to David. "It's you that's made the mistake tonight, and these people know it same as I do! They know this church was fine before you came, and they know that IF IT AIN'T BROKE . . ."

He turned to gather support from the members of his posse, but they had dropped the sign on the floor and were now seated with the rest of the silent congregation. His words hung in the air, unheeded.

" . . . don't fix it," Fred replied when he realized he was alone. He turned to look one last time in David's direction, but his vision was blurred by hot, stinging tears of frustration.

Few were willing to be caught up in his struggle now. All the politicking he had done in recent days succeeded in drawing only a handful of people. Without another word, he walked out of the sanctuary and was lost in the deepening shadows of the night.

David left the podium and started to follow after the deacon when a strong hand restrained him.

"Let him go." It was Ralph Nicholson, whose softly spoken words were picked up by the podium microphone so that the entire congregation heard them.

David started to protest but was quickly cut off.

"I was wrong before," said the big man, sadly, "but I'm not wrong now."

"He's right, David," called Dr. Newcomb from below. "Fred's in God's hands now, and there's nothing more that you can do but pray."

The old pastor began to walk toward the pulpit stairs; but after only a few steps he swooned alarmingly and grasped the pew next to him. David and Ralph were at his side in an instant (along with Mary, who seemed to have appeared out of thin air) and both were amazed to see the change that had taken place in him.

Gone was the fiery prophet with a voice of thunder. In his place stooped an old man leaning heavily on the cane his wife had given him.

"Don't mind me, gentlemen," said Dr. Newcomb once Ralph and David had helped him sit in the front row. And then he added more loudly, "Besides, don't we have some business to finish?" After saying this, he gestured over his shoulder to the congregation, which was still buzzing over Fred's uprising and retreat.

David walked back up to the podium to address the crowd.

"Well, folks," he began with a wry smile, "our first

lamppost was a real doozey!" Spontaneous laughter filled the room, and some of the tension was dispelled.

"I'm sure the next few signposts will go a little faster," he added.

Several members of the congregation voiced their approval at this suggestion, and David once again directed them to the PowerPoint display behind him, which still showed the picture of a street-sign labeled:

REDISCOVER OUR PURPOSE

"I'm going to ask Ralph Nicholson to come back to the podium. Almost six weeks ago, Ralph read article two of our constitution to the elders and deacons. The Lord spoke to our hearts through Ralph and his baritone voice. I want to give him the opportunity to do the same for you."

With copy in hand, Ralph read each purpose statement slowly but with heartfelt emotion. The people were no less affected by the words and the deep sincerity in which they were spoken than the church leaders were the first time they had heard Ralph. Emotions remained sky-high, and the reading succeeded in moving the congregation from a righteous indignation toward Fred to complete awe toward Dr. Newcomb and the papers he had penned so long ago. For many people, this moment was their first understanding of the reasons why

Midland Church exists. The lights went on everywhere in people's minds and questions began to form.

Why do we not know these things? How did we get so far away? Is it possible to go back?

David could see their perplexity and he sought to encourage the people by saying, "We did move away as a church from our core purpose, but I have good news. We can all take hold and make it ours again tonight!"

Midland Church was not a shouting church by any stretch of the imagination, but that night God's people came alive with passion. All vanity was thrown to the wind along with cultural restraint and tradition. The good people of Midland Church got involved. Somewhere that evening they took ownership, and Midland Church really became their church.

"Ushers, are you still there?" asked David, squinting toward the rear of the sanctuary. Immediately the head usher popped into view and gathered the others, who then began passing out another sheet of paper to the congregation. As he made his way down the aisle, it was clear that the head usher had been inspired by Dr. Newcomb's courage.

"The ushers are handing out an abbreviated version of article two." The street sign on the big screen behind David was replaced by a copy of that document.

"This was developed by the elders and deacons and

is basically a shortened version of Dr. Newcomb's constitution. Please take a moment and read through it."

The congregation moved to the task at hand, and each member read the following words:

Midland Church exists as a community of believers that will strive to:

1. Worship God
2. Evangelize our community and the world
3. Disciple believers to become more like Jesus Christ
4. Reach out and care for our community through acts of service
5. Individually take the Gospel of Jesus Christ into Midland

David pointed to the screen and said, "The leadership team of Midland Church encourages each of you to memorize all five points. By doing so there will never be any doubt in your mind why Midland Church is here. Fair enough?" Amens reverberated around the room.

"Dr. Newcomb, is article two of the Midland Church constitution as true today as it was almost 40 years ago?" David asked.

"Yes, David, it is," said the elder statesman as he rose slowly to his feet. "Mary and I came here because the people were lost and needed to hear about Jesus and eternal life—and God appointed us as the ones to tell them.

"I recognize a lot of faces here tonight," he continued, "and I know that Mary and I prayed with many of you and helped you to understand the message of the gospel. I can assure you that we have had no greater joy in life than those moments, and I hope that you will join your pastor now and continue the work we started. If you do, the Lord may well honor your step of faith and pour out a great blessing."

After speaking, the old pastor met the eyes of several men and women he recognized and gave them a kindly smile, then sat down again, satisfied.

"Pastor Newcomb may be close to 80," said Pastor David, laughing, "but he can still preach, can't he?" This was greeted by a wave of laughter from the crowd, and a whole new burst of applause.

It was time to move on to the next signpost. With the appropriate gesture from David, the technician moved to the next slide. A picture of a lighthouse appeared on the wall.

Several "Oohs" and "Ahs" floated out of the congregation in response to this, and David smiled like a proud parent. He had labored long and hard, with the help of Terry Sullivan, to find the perfect visual expression of his vision, and he was very happy with the result. The picture showed a raging storm descending on a stretch of rocky coastline, complete with crashing waves, sinister clouds and a lightning bolt slicing through the top left corner.

And of course, standing tall and proud in the middle of it all, was the lighthouse. It was painted a stark white with a red cross in the middle that seemed to defy the storm. The structure of it was almost cone-shaped, with the base much wider than the top, and was crowned by the light that sent a piercing beam through the darkness around it.

"This is my vision for our church," said Pastor David, taking another opportunity to look behind him and admire the illustration. "This brings us to the second signpost." From out of the corner of the screen came marching letters that formed the words:

RETURN TO THE ORIGINAL VISION

"Let me make a clarification between the first signpost and the second signpost," David pointed out. "Understanding our God-given purpose is fundamental to who we are and where we are going as a church, and it is outlined in the Great Commission. It's the foundation on which all ministry must be built and sustained. Vision rises from that very place. Daniel and Mary Newcomb knew long ago the purpose and potential of a local New Testament church. They willingly placed themselves before the Lord as vessels of service to go anywhere the Lord led.

"God led them to Midland, where something altogether marvelous happened. As Dr. Newcomb contemplated his calling to plant a church in Midland, he recognized the formidable challenge ahead. They had never planted a church before. Foremost on his mind was the question, Lord, what does this look like? Now we all know that James tells us that if anyone lacks wisdom, he should ask the Lord. That's just what our founding pastor did. And God began to fill his heart with love for the people in Midland. That love turned into a personal reality check. Dr. Newcomb thought, 'If I really love the people of Midland, no sacrifice will be too great in my pursuit of their souls.'

"As Dr. Newcomb stayed focused on his love for Christ and the spiritual needs of the people he had come to reach, a startling image of a lighthouse formed in his mind one day. The light went out far and wide. Many people saw the light and they were saved from destruction. Ladies and gentlemen, that was the original vision Dr. Newcomb had for this church and this city.

"Now stay with me," Pastor David urged. "This is the really exciting part. Dr. Newcomb's vision for Midland Church is just as real and valuable to us today as it was the day it entered his heart!

"No matter what is going on around us, we are called to be a shining light to our community. We will stand strong as a refuge for the lost in the middle of any storm, and we will expose the dangers of sin through the light of God's truth. That is our mission."

He paused to allow his words to sink in, then continued.

"This brings us to the third and final lamppost for this evening. It is the express desire of the elders and deacons to invite all to the church altar for a special dedication."

Instantly, new words formed on the wall. They read:

REDEDICATE THE CHURCH FAMILY

"As you can see," said David, "your leaders have already made a commitment to carry this through. Tonight I am asking all of you to do the same. If you are willing to join us in returning Midland Church to its rightful place as a kingdom lighthouse, then I would ask you to come up to the front so that we can all dedicate this bold step of faith together."

The congregation stirred and for several minutes the aisles were full of parishioners on their way to the church altar. David had already planted himself on his knees in front of the altar, and one by one the people of the Midland Church found a place to kneel.

In the end, the entire congregation huddled humbly together at the front of the sanctuary, and for almost an hour the people spontaneously lifted their voices in unity. Looking back several years later, most of those people would refer to that night as a revival. But David always considered it an awakening—an evening when the people of God broke out of comfortable slumber and proclaimed Midland Church as a lighthouse whose greatest years were yet to come.

"What a night!" exclaimed David to his wife when the congregation had all gone home. The two of them were sitting in the front pew eating ice-cream cones that Catherine had bought from Dairy Queen while her husband and Ralph cleaned up.

"You did great," she said, putting her head on his shoulder and sighing contentedly.

"Everyone did great," he replied, shaking his head. "I'm almost sorry it's all over!"

Hearing this, Catherine lifted up her head and playfully touched her cone against his in a frozen toast.

CHAPTER 13

Community at Last

*T*here is no such thing as a perfect church.

This is a popular statement among pastors these days and very often finds its way into the middle of Sunday morning sermons. When it does, it is frequently accompanied by a punchline that goes something like this: "If you ever do find yourself in the middle of a perfect church, get out as quickly as you can! The only thing you can do in such a place is mess everything up."

In the many years following the rebirth of Midland Church, a great deal of people found their way into the middle of its congregation, and of course none of them found it to be perfect. However, a large majority of them did find it to be a wonderfully exciting place and were very thankful for the imperfections, because they wanted to stay!

And so the congregation grew—both in number and in maturity. With Pastor David at the helm, the church fought through seasons of adversity to accomplish mighty things for the glory of God. It became a Kingdom Lighthouse and remains one to this day— built upon the solid Rock and bursting with the light of truth for all to see.

However, if you have been paying attention to this story, then of course you know there is something missing—some sign on the horizon that has yet to be unveiled. It is the final—and perhaps most important—piece to our little puzzle.

⚜

"Okay, everyone," called Pastor David from the old microphone at the front of the gym. "We're gonna get started in a couple of minutes and there's only a few dishes left at the dessert table, so let's finish 'em off!" A cheerful cry of approval rose up from the crowd in response to this and was quickly drowned out by the sound of several tennis shoes squeaking across the floor.

Pastor David stepped back from the microphone for a moment and watched his flock with a satisfied grin. He still looked very young, but his face was already becoming chiseled with that particular mix of patience and exasperation that only comes from ministering to people on a regular basis. His gaze was steady, his posture confident and he was dressed in what would later become his trademark classic casual style (this outfit had already garnered him the nickname "Hip Dave").

After a few seconds, he stepped down from the makeshift stage and walked over to his own table, where Catherine was waiting for him with what was already her trademark cheerful smile. She was dressed in bright colors and also looked very young, although her stomach bulged slightly with the wonderful potential of future joy.

"Is everything ready?" David asked her after a quick kiss.

"Just give me the signal," she replied, and then was struck by a wonderful new thought: *Does this mean that I get to eat dessert for two?*

Twenty minutes later, the 160 members of the Midland congregation made their way to the sanctuary and settled into pews with satisfied tummies. They were an encouragingly diverse group of people—young, old, minorities, majorities, men, women—and yet they were all extremely comfortable with one another and happy to be together. Several of them—especially many of the older members—were wearing black.

"All right," began Pastor David with a smile, "as most of you know . . ." His voice trailed off as he spotted Catherine slowly walking down the middle aisle with an elderly lady holding on to her arm. This woman wore a long pink dress that seemed to warm the air around her, although a black hat crowned her head and a small veil shadowed her eyes.

"Hello, Mary," said Pastor David, tenderly. He smiled when she looked up at him, and yet the corners of his mouth were pulled down ever so slightly by two little anchors of grief. "Thank you so much for coming."

"Pastor David," Mary replied with a strong voice, "we are here to celebrate my husband, and I wouldn't miss that for the world!" The congregation—which had risen to its feet out of respect the moment Pastor David had said Mary's name—murmured approvingly at this. As the two women made their way toward the front of the sanctuary, the people radiated encouragement and warmth like gentle waves lapping against a quiet, sandy beach.

Bathed in such a sense of fellowship, Mary stood a little taller and seemed a little stronger as she reached the front pew and sat down with Catherine. The crowd quickly did the same, and Pastor David continued.

"As most of you know," he said, still smiling but

with a voice full of emotion, "it has been two years since the reawakening of our church, and we have chosen this day as a review session to see how our congregation has been living up to our church covenant." He briefly gestured to a large framed document on the wall behind him and to the left, which contained a large number of signatures.

"This event was planned long ago," he continued. "However, our plans were shaken up quite a bit last week when Dr. Newcomb went home to be with the Lord." Pastor David's voice choked with emotion as he said the old man's name, and the congregation whispered sympathetically when he stepped back from the microphone to gather his composure. Ever since the night of the reawakening Dr. Newcomb had taken the younger man under his wing as a spiritual father does, and the two had become very close.

David looked down at the front row in an attempt to deliver some comfort to the recent widow. However, he was not surprised when her serene and peaceful face comforted him instead.

"I have to confess that my first reaction was to cancel today's event," he said and then looked back down at Mary with a strange kind of smile. "But after talking to those who knew him best, I was convinced that Dr. Newcomb would have been totally against such a thing." He continued to look at Mary as he said this, and she quietly winked at him in response.

"So instead," said David, "today's mission is twofold. First, we are going to celebrate the life of a godly man. And second, we're going to examine the church that he started and make sure he is proud of the way we're running it whenever he looks down from heaven!"

The crowd spontaneously rose to its feet and applauded. Unable to speak any longer, David pointed to Ralph Nicholson (still manning his post at the improved sound booth) and stepped off the stage to give Mary Newcomb the warmest hug he could offer.

Almost instantly a white screen lowered itself from the ceiling and a slide show began that detailed the life and accomplishments of Dr. Daniel Newcomb. It was a powerful time for everyone, especially for those who had known the old saint the longest, and it ended with three-quarters of the congregation wiping joyful tears out of their eyes. An open forum followed in which people were encouraged to share their stories and memories of Dr. Newcomb, and well over an hour passed before Ralph Nicholson decided that it was time to get down to business.

"I was here when Dr. Newcomb started this church," said Ralph, standing at the main podium. "It breaks my heart that we let things get outta whack after he retired." Those in the crowd who had been members for longer than two years looked down at their laps.

"But I thank God ev'ry day that He gave us a second chance." Ralph's eyes blazed as he said, "So let's make sure we haven't been wastin' it."

The congregation cheered heartily in reply, and the other elders and deacons made their way down the aisles and formed a group on the side of the stage.

One by one, each man delivered a short presentation on the various ministries under his supervision and detailed the different plans and visions for the future. A question-and-answer time followed each presentation and allowed members of the congregation to clear up any confusing issues and concerns and speak their mind on a variety of matters. Ralph mediated the entire event and wasted no opportunity to encourage what was working—or spur on those activities and leaders that seemed to be loitering in the caboose.

David watched the whole thing from the sidelines— a strange mix of anxiety and relief covering his face—and said very little.

Terry Sullivan had been slated for the final presentation. As the young deacon made his way to the microphone, David looked over and nodded to his wife, and the two of them quietly slipped out the back of the sanctuary.

"We have been having some very exciting times in our Awana ministry," Terry began after adjusting the podium microphone. "I guess I'll just start with the numbers." He shuffled through a stack of papers in his hand, and coughed politely before continuing.

"When I began as the Commander two years ago, we averaged about 20 kids attending Awana every Wednesday night. Our attendance at the final ceremony last week was 182 children."

The crowd buzzed excitedly at these words, and Terry waited a few moments before continuing.

"Two years ago, we had 12 adults trained as Awana leaders; now we have 47." The audience began to buzz again but Terry held his hand up, knowing that things were only going to get more impressive. "The great thing about our leaders today is that 11 of them are high school students who have chosen to serve the younger children, and 12 are adults who don't even have kids in the Awana program!

"Another very important facet of the Awana ministry is that it has opened a lot of other doors for different activities on Wednesday nights. For example, a large number of small groups have moved to Wednesdays because, in addition to being a great ministry for kids, Awana basically provides the childcare that allows the parents to meet together and study the Word of God."

"How far have we developed this childcare thing?" broke in Ralph, who had not been aware of it and was very excited about the potential.

"Well," replied Terry, confidently, "not very far, I

suppose. Right now groups are just doing this on their own because it makes sense. But nothing has been officially set up yet by the deacons or the staff." This comment elicited a large round of chatter from the congregation, and after a few minutes, Ralph broke in again to get things back on track.

"I'll make a presentation at the next elder's meeting," Ralph said, "and we'll make sure we milk this all we can. Go ahead, Terry."

"Thanks, Ralph," Terry replied. "We have developed one ministry that I'm very eager to pursue even further—and that's witnessing to the parents who bring their kids to Awana but don't come to church."

In the back of the sanctuary, a young man and a young woman quietly slipped through the double doors carrying large, bulky bundles. Ralph saw them and shivered as a wave of déjà-vu swept through him momentarily.

"At first," continued Terry, "the parents would just drop off their kids in the parking lot and then pick them up in the same place; however, we felt like that might be a little dangerous for the kids (his eyes twinkled as he relayed this idea) and so we now require that all parents walk their children into the gym. This way, the kids are safe and we get to meet their folks and introduce ourselves." A wave of approving nods rolled through the congregation at this creative idea.

"Then," Terry went on, "one of our leaders came up with the great idea of starting a coffee bar in one of the classrooms downstairs. So now we have about 30 parents who hang out together and socialize while their kids learn about Jesus."

"Do we have any plans to witness to these parents?" inquired Ralph.

"Well," said Terry, "Pastor David has been spending a lot of time getting to know them all, and they talk about what the kids are learning, but no official program is in place." Several of the audience members joined in the discussion at this point and threw out a wide variety of suggestions. After a quick show of hands, it was decided that a biblical parenting class would begin on Wednesday nights for anyone who desired to attend.

"All that's left," finished Terry, "is to make my weekly plea. We still need more help! Our program is growing by leaps and bounds, and I ask all of you to please consider becoming Awana leaders, or at least to consider coming out on Wednesday nights and listening to your kids say verses. It's really a lot of fun!"

Having finished his presentation, Terry began to walk down the stairs leading from the pulpit. About halfway down, a loud voice rang out from the rear of the sanctuary.

"Ladies and gentlemen," said the voice. The congregation rolled around as one body to get a look at the speaker. Some of them were reminded of that painfully exciting night two years before, but the connection quickly faded as Pastor David stepped out of the shadows. He was carrying what appeared to be two large street signs in his hands, and the smile on his face may have been considered crazed if the people didn't know him.

"Does anybody remember the Five Signposts?" he asked, waggling his eyebrows suggestively. The congregation babbled excitedly in remembrance of the aforementioned evening, especially when Catherine stepped into the light carrying three more street signs.

There was one exception to this babbling, however, and that was Terry Sullivan. He had been caught once again by Pastor David's interruption and was awkwardly perched on one of the stairs at the front of the sanctuary. He had an extremely puzzled look on his face. Something about the "Five Signposts" just didn't seem right . . .

"Since we're examining the progress of our church," continued David, "I thought it might be a good idea if we reviewed the steps that helped to get us turned around. Everybody ready?" The congregation prattled and nodded vigorously in response to this—except again for Terry, who sat down on one of the stairs and began to rub his forehead with an even more puzzled expression.

"What was the first step?" called David from the back.

"Rediscover our purpose . . ." was meekly suggested by four or five individuals who had discerned that David wanted an audible response. The pastor frowned and wagged his finger back and forth.

"We have to do better than that!" he cried. "Now . . . what's the first step?"

"REDISCOVER OUR PURPOSE!!!" roared the crowd in response, now that they understood.

"Very good," said David, holding up the appropriate street sign. "And what's the second step?"

"RETURN TO THE ORIGINAL VISION!!!" cried the crowd. David was satisfied and didn't feel like he needed to explain the concept of "original vision" in detail, since he had just finished a sermon series on it the week before.

"Okay," he continued, "and number three?"

"REDEDICATE THE CHURCH FAMILY!!!" called the congregation. This time, Catherine held up one of her signs for all to see.

"That was by far the strangest and most wonderful night of my life," mused Pastor David in a softer voice, but then he let out a startled "YOUP!!" as Catherine pinched him from behind.

"Uhhhh, right . . ." he corrected himself sheepishly. "I mean the second most wonderful night . . ."

Catherine smiled in reply and motioned for David to continue. The crowd received a great deal of pleasure from this interchange, and almost everyone was laughing . . . except for Terry Sullivan. He was still sitting down but was now counting something on his fingers as if he were an elementary student trying to decide how many apples were left over in a particularly vexing equation.

"All righty," continued Pastor David, "and what's number . . ."

"FOUR!!!" cried Terry Sullivan, suddenly popping back up to his feet. In the process, he also popped back into microphone range and sent an ear-shattering wave of feedback through the sound system and out the speakers. The entire congregation gasped at the volume of it and rolled their heads to look at the young deacon . . . who in turn was staring at Pastor David in disbelief.

"You only told us four!" cried Terry. Pastor David smiled as the congregation swiveled back to look at him. He shrugged his shoulders nonchalantly.

"What do you mean, Terry?"

"There are Five Signposts!" replied the deacon, still working things through in his own head. "But you only told us about four of them. You never mentioned the fifth signpost!"

"Do you remember what the fourth signpost is?" asked Pastor David.

"Of course," said Terry, "it's 'Reorganize Our Approach to the Community,' which we're doing—but you didn't tell us the fifth one, did you?"

"No, I didn't," confessed Pastor David. "But I'm ready to unveil it today . . . and here it is." As he spoke, he gestured to Catherine, who then raised up one of the street signs in front of her. The top of it was green, and it looked the same as any other street sign except for the fact that the lettering was much larger. On it was written only one word: **REMEMBER.**

Once again a wave of conversation broke over the congregation and the people began to wildly discuss everything that had happened. After a few minutes, Pastor David called for attention in order to explain.

"The Fifth Signpost," he said, "is the most critical one for us to work on now. Just like Ralph said earlier, we have to remember our heritage—both the fruit of our victories and the barrenness of our mistakes—in order to keep us on the course of our vision. Most important, we need to remember how we got turned around so that we can keep our momentum going. Does everyone understand?" The people nodded their heads. Pastor David couldn't help but chuckle at their enthusiasm.

"So," he continued, with a sly look in Catherine's direction, "my wife and I have put together three ways in which our church can actively remember the events of the past two years. The first is through the legacy of a great man."

After saying this he nodded at Catherine, who had positioned herself underneath the very back wall of the sanctuary, between the two sets of double doors. A large plaque, which had been covered by a small sheet and unseen by the congregation beforehand, was hanging on the middle of the wall. Catherine tugged on the rope connected to the sheet and revealed the following words inscribed in large, bold and black letters:

DR. DANIEL NEWCOMB MEMORIAL SANCTUARY

Under the letters was a rough sketch of the late pastor's face, which was kind and gentle even when carved into stone. The congregation went wild upon seeing this and cheered and applauded fervently.

Having been told about David's plan before the evening began, Mary Newcomb had made her way slowly to the back in order to see the unveiling. When the curtain was lifted and she saw her husband's tender face once again, a single tear rolled down her cheek. "I love you, Daniel," she whispered. Nobody around her saw the tear, and nobody heard her voice . . . which was exactly how she wanted it.

"What's more," Pastor David continued, "every year the congregation of this church will meet on this specific day to accomplish what we have accomplished this evening. We will celebrate this wonderful man—and the church he planted—and evaluate ourselves to make sure that we never waste the opportunity he has given us through God's power." Another round of applause exploded from the congregation, and now Mary joined in with all of the energy she could funnel into her shaking hands.

"Now for the Signposts," said David. He handed them to Ralph Nicholson, who began to set them up along the back wall. "These will be permanently installed in the church as a reminder of where we have come from . . . and where we are going."

The congregation "ooooooooed" and "aaaahed" over each sign and several people touched them reverently. This went on for several minutes, and things had just begun to quiet down a little bit when a mischievous sparkle flashed across Pastor David's eyes.

"I have one more surprise," he called out to the congregation. "Would you like to know what it is?" Several members called back yes in response and craned their necks to see where the Pastor had hidden it.

"Follow me," David said simply. He then turned on his heels and jogged out of the sanctuary and into the parking lot. Bewildered, the crowd of people followed as quickly as it could, until all 160 members were standing in the middle of the road at the intersection of 9th and Kearney.

"Could someone please read our church sign for me?" asked Pastor David once everyone had quieted down. Several people tried, squinting and shading their eyes, until they realized that a large cloth was now covering the placard.

Pastor David watched them and a peculiar smile stretched across his face. When Catherine saw it, she knew that her husband was thinking fondly of a dusty stranger in faded jeans and a white cowboy hat.

"Okay, Ralph!" called the pastor once the attention of the crowd had focused on the sign. The big man stepped out from behind the sign and pulled the sheet away.

For a few moments there was only silence. People gaped and gawked and put their hands up to their mouths in pure astonishment. Then—all of a sudden and all at once—the gapers and gawkers found their voices once again and cried out in a single, involuntary rush of approval, "WOW!!!"

The sign had been painted in full color, and it depicted a ferocious storm surrounding a rocky outcropping along a sandy beach. The unmoving waves crashed and frothed with foam . . . the unseen wind howled and heaved itself against the rocks . . . and the stationary streak of lightning tore its way across the sky. And, of course, standing confidently in the middle of it all was the lighthouse.

The cylinder of this building was a radiant white and seemed stubbornly clean against the fury of the storm. Its base was not built upon the foundation rock, so to speak, but instead seemed to be growing out of it like an iron tree.

But the true glory of the picture was the light. It sat atop the cylinder like a crown and was unaffected by the raging scene surrounding it as it burned a beam of light out into the lost and lonely night. This beam then gathered a streak of color and swooped itself into the first line of a large M, which began the words "Midland Church." These letters were scrawled across the middle of the sign, yet they almost seemed inconsequential in comparison to the glory and splendor of the light.

In smaller, scripted letters, the following words were sketched along the bottom:

I am the Way, and the Truth, and the Light.

"This is my vision," said Catherine and Pastor David.

"This is my duty," said Ralph Nicholson.

"This is our mission," said the congregation.

And they were all correct.

PART TWO

The Five Signposts at Work

Rediscover Our Purpose

*Searching for the purpose Christ has for
your church can counter the seemingly
inevitable slide toward spiritual entropy.*

One of the most observable principles of
physics is the law of entropy, which states
that things left to themselves will degenerate
and become useless. Unfortunately, the Church as an
institution has historically been a reliable place to
observe this law in action. For example, a telling passage
in 2 Kings 22 highlights the "spiritual entropy" that
plagued the Israelites throughout the Old Testament.
In this chapter, we find the Temple in disrepair—literally falling apart to the degree that young King Josiah
imports new stones and timber for its restoration.

However, in the middle of the rebuilding project, an amazing discovery is made: the Book of the Law of God.

Apparently the religious leaders of the time had kept the day-to-day activities of the Temple running while the Living Word of God collected dust on some obscure shelf—unused and forgotten. In other words, the residents of Jerusalem had continued to observe the ceremonies and traditions of worship without even knowing why they were doing it. They had lost their purpose.

Sadly, many of today's churches are experiencing a similar situation. No longer rooted in the Great Commission, they have gradually succumbed to the attacks of entropy and have fallen into a rut of useless activity. These attacks—so often unseen and unfelt—come from a wide variety of sources, but the following are among the most common:

- *Satan.* The Great Commission embodies all that Satan hates and fears and so he will do everything in his power to destroy a Kingdom Lighthouse. Using the pride, fear and greed of individuals, he subtly bends the focus of a congregation inward, until it can only see itself.
- *Division.* The interests, experiences and cultural views of individual members, while positive for a congregation in terms of diversity, will hollow it out from the inside if there is no

unifying purpose.

- *Sin.* When it is not dealt with biblically, the sin of individuals—especially church leaders—will tarnish the "light of the world" until it is cold, and dim and ineffective.

These are the forces that eroded the nation of Israel, as well as the good people of Midland Church, and they are still at work today. However, the good news is that these forces are not insurmountable. The discovery of the Book of the Law in 2 Kings led to a renewed sense of purpose and a nationwide revival. The unearthing of a tattered Church Constitution started the good people of Midland Church down a path toward restoration. And a reinvigorated focus on the Great Commission can provide any church with a worthwhile purpose—to go and reach its community with the gospel of Jesus Christ.

Return to the Original Vision

Take an active step by reshaping your original purpose into clear, compelling words that can be adopted and applied by all.

Have you ever experienced a "self-service" church? On the outside, these types of churches are hard to distinguish from other churches unless you know what to look for: a lack of fruit. These churches seek out volunteers, raise money and sponsor activities; but it seems as if their only goal in going through these motions today is to ensure that they will be able to go through them again tomorrow. In other words, their sole purpose for engaging in Christianity is to further the cause of Christianity, not to further the cause of God and bring Him glory through fulfilling His Great Commission.

As was the case with the good people of Midland Church, the transition from a Kingdom Lighthouse into a self-service institution usually takes time and is rooted in a disconnect between the original vision of the founders and the everyday lives of the current members. Just like King Josiah, Pastor David was fortunate enough to stumble across a document that was filled with the truths of God. However, this was only the first step.

In order to reconnect Dr. Newcomb's original vision with Midland Church's current congregation, Pastor David needed to reformat that vision in a way that was clear and applicable to his flock. In other words, Dr. Newcomb's Church Constitution provided a solid foundation, but Pastor David and the other church leaders still needed to build a modern house.

Of course, there is good news and bad news here for today's churches that wish to return to their original vision. The good news is that all churches are required by the government to form a constitution, which includes a purpose statement. The bad news is that founding pastors often do not spend a great deal of time writing these, which results in a "boilerplate" constitution—a copy of another church's constitution, which was copied from another church, and so on.

However, even the most meager Church Constitution will provide a rough outline for moving forward.

In addition, we all have Scripture to fall back on, and the Great Commission provides support for even the shakiest of foundations. In the end, it will take energy and effort to revitalize the vision of a tired institution, but doing so is a necessary step to revitalize the members of that institution and transform them into a Kingdom Lighthouse that will ultimately bring glory to God.

Rededicate the Church Family

All the members of a Body must covenant to work together before positive steps can be taken and momentum established.

Nature abhors a vacuum and will seek to fill it with anything available. Similarly, no church really exists without a purpose. The problem is that so many churches today, like Midland Church, simply have the wrong purpose. The good people of Midland Church were certainly sincere and dedicated about maintaining the activities of their church; however, the purpose behind their sincerity and dedication was to make themselves comfortable. The church was slowly dragged away from its original vision, which created a vacuum, and that vacuum was quickly filled with whatever was most convenient and enjoyable.

But why did it all happen so easily? Why didn't anyone realize what was going on and throw up a red flag? There are two reasons. First, the Bible says that we Christians are like sheep, and sheep follow their leaders. Second, every church has at least one antagonist; a poor leader. In the case of Midland Church, it was Fred Turner—a sincere, hard-working deacon whose understanding of the church's purpose was born not out of the Bible but out of a combination of bad experiences, personal pain and a strong conviction about the way things ought to be.

Whether it is the oldest member of a church, the strongest personality or the largest donor, we must identify and deal with those people who are leading falsely, because we can be sure that others will follow. Of course, one effective way to identify these individuals (as in the case of Fred Turner) is to note how they react to change—usually they will be very resistant to it, even to a positive change back to the original vision. While we can sympathize with their struggle to leave what is comfortable, we must not allow them to prevail. Our calling is to fear the Lord, not man, and that calling should force us to firmly confront those who oppose God's design for His Church.

Once the antagonists have been identified and dealt with biblically, the pastor will then face the challenge of convincing the rank-and-file members that their church must change. Once again, this process can be taxing, especially because it is impractical to move a large flock of sheep one at a time. However, the rewards of this rededication are immeasurable in terms of the joy that is generated when the Body of Christ moves in unison and brings glory to its Head.

Reorganize Our Approach to the Community

The church must take an honest look at the
community surrounding it and eliminate
any blind spots.

Not many years ago, the U.S. Department of Transportation estimated that there were 19,000 accidents and as many as 6,000 deaths on America's roadways due to "blind spots" in a driver's vision.[1] Simply put, a blind spot is an area that drivers think they can see, when in reality they cannot. These are dangerous on the road, but even more dangerous in a church.

All too often, a local church will have a serious blind spot when it comes to the community surrounding it, causing a glaring omission in that church's present and future plans. These churches often wonder why they don't encounter more visitors and why those who do visit choose not to stay. They assume that the community will know and appreciate their church's existence because it has a steeple, or an electric sign, or even a Yellow-Pages advertisement—but that simply isn't the case. These churches feel that they are doing everything they can to encourage evangelism, but they have a blind spot. They just don't see what they're missing.

The same can be said about Pastor David and the rest of Midland Church. Nobody in the congregation (except maybe Fred Turner) was actively opposed to evangelism and bringing in new faces, and yet nobody in the congregation tried to actively engage the community. In many ways, the congregation wasn't even aware that they were supposed to do this. They had a blind spot and their light was dimmed. Even worse, the members of Midland Church were inward-focused, which meant that whatever light did shine out from their actions and activities only illuminated the inside of the church, leaving those outside with no idea that the light even existed.

Therefore, churches with a blind spot must reorganize their approach to the community and must do so using the examples of those who got it right. For example, in Acts 2, after the anointing of the Holy

Spirit at Pentecost, the followers of Jesus were emboldened to take their message to the streets using different languages to make sure they would be heard. They did not care that they were made fun of and ignored by some; they only cared that they were noticed, were given a chance to proclaim the good news, and were used by God to save the community around them. They had no blind spot.

Peter and John preached in the Temple, Paul made tents and taught in the synagogues, and Jesus performed miracles on the street. The common denominator between each of these individuals is that being noticed was a prerequisite of being useful, and the same is true of our churches today. We must not have a blind spot. We must reorganize our approach to the community so that people know we are there and care about the community. If that doesn't happen, our community will not care about us.

Note

1. "New Technology Prevents Blind-Spot Accidents," *The Bridge*, January/March 2001, v. 15, n. 2.

Remember

**Continually remembering, repenting
and redoing your church's vision is
essential for its vitality.**

God expects us to remember. Throughout the Scriptures, He continually exhorts us to remember our experiences with Him, both good and bad. For example, the Israelites were commanded to remember the miracles of God through feasts and celebrations, such as the ceremony of Passover and the Feast of Booths (see Exod. 12:21-27; Deut. 16:13). Similarly, in the book of Revelation, Jesus chastises the church at Ephesus because its people had forgotten their first love (see Rev. 2:4). Indeed, the old axiom is true that those who forget the past are doomed to repeat it.

It is important to note that this type of spiritual memory is different from human memory. It bears no resemblance to a middle-aged man looking back at his glory days on the football field. Instead, this spiritual memory is focused on the present and the future. In other words, the primary function of spiritual memory is to relocate an original vision in order to adjust the present and prepare for the future.

Many members of Midland Church had experienced the glory days of Dr. Newcomb and his original vision. They knew what it felt like to shine their light proudly into the community and see fruit arise from their efforts. But after it all ended, they forgot. They didn't remember how good it felt to be used by God, so they didn't strive to be used by God again. Only when Pastor David stumbled upon the old Church Constitution did their memories stir—and along with them a longing for something better.

But of course, remembering the past is only the first step. After we remember, we must adjust what we are currently doing; and in order to do that, we must repent. This was Jesus' command to the church at Ephesus: They must repent of their sin in order to get back to their first love (see Rev. 2:5). And this is what we must repent of: our sin. We must admit that we have abandoned God's purpose for the Church and we must commit to falling back in line with Him. It is also important to note that one individual can only repent for his own sin—not the sin of an entire church. Therefore, a corporate remembrance of a church must lead to a corporate repentance by the church.

By remembering the past, we can repent in the present, and then we must redo in the future. This was also Jesus' command to the church at Ephesus: They must once again do the first works. It is important to understand that Jesus is not simply talking about going through the motions again. He's talking about taking all of the activity and energy of the church and filling it with love and a desire to do His will.

This is why Pastor David by himself was unable to figure out what was wrong with Midland Church. He could sense that things were off, but he was too close to all of the activities and buzz in the church to understand that these things were empty. It took someone from the outside to show him that the activities had no purpose. Only then was he able to lead the church in remembering the original vision of Dr. Newcomb, lead them in repentance, and then lead them in starting over again with a proper purpose, light and life.

In addition to remembering our first love, we must also remember the times we failed, especially as a church. In order to escape the mistakes of our past we must never forget them, and we must unashamedly hang them on our steeples so that we can see the pit out of

which we were saved. In other words, we must constant-
ly celebrate our church's history—warts and all—in order
to keep the vision alive by recalling the good along with
the bad. This is what it means to remember.

A quote from A. W. Tozer sums up the salient
points of this epilogue:

> There is scarcely anything so dull and mean-
> ingless as Bible doctrine taught for its own
> sake. Truth divorced from life is not truth in its
> Biblical sense, but something else and some-
> thing less. . . . No man is better for knowing
> that God in the beginning created the heavens
> and the earth. The devil knows that, and so did
> Ahab and Judas Iscariot. No man is better for
> knowing that God so loved the world of men
> that he gave his only begotten Son to die for
> their redemption. In hell there are millions
> who know that. Theological truth is useless
> until it is obeyed. The purpose behind all doc-
> trine is to secure moral action.[1]

The Five Signposts in this book are all based on
biblical doctrine—and yet they are all words. I am afraid
to say that this experience (my writing the words and
your reading them) will be entirely a waste if they
remain nothing to you but words, even if they are inter-

esting or provocative words. Let these words become actions. Your church can be restored to its rightful place as a powerful Lighthouse for the kingdom of God if you are willing to take a step of moral action, get on the road and follow the signs.

Note

1. A. W. Tozer, *Of God and Men: Cultivating the Divine Human Relationship* (Camp Hill, PA: Christian Publications, 1995), p. 23.

More Ways for Churches to Move Up and Reach Out

Extreme Church Makeover
A Biblical Plan to Help Your Church Achieve Unity and Freedom in Christ
Neil T. Anderson and Charles Mylander
Hardcover • ISBN 08307.37944

Changing Church
How God Is Leading His Church into the Future
C. Peter Wagner
Hardcover • ISBN 08307.32780

The Habits of Highly Effective Churches
Being Strategic in Your God-Given Ministry
George Barna
Paperback • ISBN 08307.18605

The Five-Star Church
Serving God and His People with Excellence
Stan Toler and Alan Nelson
Paperback • ISBN 08307.23501

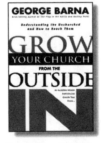

Grow Your Church from the Outside In
Understanding the Unchurched and How to Reach Them
George Barna
Hardcover • ISBN 08307.30877

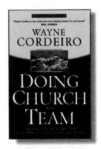

Doing Church as a Team
The Miracle of Teamwork and How It Transforms Churches
Wayne Cordeiro
Paperback • ISBN 08307.36808

Available at Bookstores Everywhere!

Visit **www.regalbooks.com** to join **Regal's FREE e-newsletter.** You'll get useful **excerpts** from our newest releases and **special access** to online chats with your favorite authors. Sign up today!

Regal
God's Word for Your World™
www.regalbooks.com